The Tory Mind on Education
1979–94

The Tory Mind on Education
1979–94

Denis Lawton

 The Falmer Press

(A member of the Taylor & Francis Group)
London • Washington, D.C.

UK   The Falmer Press, 4 John Street, London WC1N 2ET
USA   The Falmer Press, Taylor & Francis Inc., 1900 Frost Road, Suite 101,
Bristol, PA 19007

First published in 1994

**A catalogue record for this book is available from the British
Library**

**Library of Congress Cataloging-in-Publication Data are
available on request**

ISBN 0 7507 0350 4 cased
ISBN 0 7507 0351 2 paper

Jacket design by Caroline Archer

Typeset in 11/13pt Garamond by
Graphicraft Typesetters Ltd., Hong Kong

*Printed in Great Britain by Burgess Science Press, Basingstoke on
paper which has a specified pH value on final paper manufacture
of not less than 7.5 and is therefore 'acid free'.*

Contents

List of Abbreviations

APS   Assisted Places Scheme
ASI   Adam Smith Institute
CPG   Conservative Philosophy Group
CPS   Centre for Policy Studies
DES   Department of Education and Science
DFE   Department for Education
GCE   General Certificate of Education
GCSE   General Certificate of Secondary Education
GSA   Girls' Schools Association
HMI   Her Majesty's Inspectorate
IEA   Institute of Economic Affairs
ILEA   Inner London Education Authority
IPPR   Institute of Public Policy Research
KS   Key Stage (of National Curriculum)
LEA   Local Education Authority
NCC   National Curriculum Council
NIESR National Institute for Economic and Social Research
NUT   National Union of Teachers
PSBR   Public Sector Borrowing Requirement
RSA   Royal Society of Arts
SCAA   School Curriculum and Assessment Authority
SEAC   School Examination and Assessment Council
TES   Times Educational Supplement

Preface

Part of my professional responsibility is to keep educational policies under review and try to explain them. This has been an increasingly difficult task since 1979. By the Summer of 1993, when I started writing this book, education was in a state of disarray: the National Curriculum, originally welcomed by the profession, had gone terribly wrong; teachers' morale was low and only lifted when there was a successful boycott of the flawed national tests in 1993; in addition, teachers' expertise was further threatened by proposals such as the one-year training programme for primary teachers — derisively referred to as 'mums army'.

Some of the mess was caused by mismanagement, but much of it seemed — to those involved in the education service — clearly attributable to wrong policies. It was frequently observed that, in education as in some other social areas, policies were not only driven by ideology, but ideology of a most destructive kind.

In previous books (1989 and 1992) I have explored Conservative ideology or ideologies in the context of the Education Reform Act (1988). In writing this book I do not wish to contradict those earlier views, but for some purposes I now find them insufficiently analytical to help diagnose what is wrong more generally with education in the 1990s.

The specific purpose of this book is to try to make sense of conservative education policies since 1979 by referring to beliefs, values and attitudes. To do that it will be necessary to explore various definitions of Conservativism, to detect various ideologies within the ranks of the Conservative Party — past and present — and to attempt to relate ideology to policies. One must not, of course, rule out the possibility that policies are either completely haphazard or based on short-term expediency, but, in general, it is better to assume rationality of a kind, even if it may be too optimistic to expect complete rationality.

It is also the case that ideologies change; and it is now true that a concern for the Empire and an affection for the Church of England are no longer strongly associated with the Conservative Party. But these were surface manifestations of deeper attitudes and values. I am more concerned with the deeper, long-lasting Tory views and will try to relate them to current issues in education.

Preface

The title of this book presented some difficulties. I wanted to give an account of policies since 1979, but I also wanted to try to explain these policies in terms of a philosophy or ideology. However, Conservatives claim to be free from such abstractions; but they do not deny a Conservative mentality or set of values. The 'Tory Mind' may have something in common with 'La Pensée Sauvage', but not much.

Denis Lawton
June 1994

Part I

Background

The first part of this book is intended to provide some background about the years before 1979.

Chapter 1 puts forward some definitions of Conservativism and descriptions of Tory beliefs — mainly by self-confessed Conservatives. The second section of the chapter goes on to describe traditional Conservative views on education.

Chapter 2 provides a brief outline of the years between the 1944 Education Act and 1979 when our detailed account will begin. Part of that story is the move from post-war cooperation in 1944 to the gradual breakdown of consensus in the 1960s and 1970s.

Chapter 1

Conservatism and Conservative Views on Education

In a progressive country change is constant; and the question is not whether you should resist change which is inevitable but whether that change should be carried out in deference to the manners, the customs, the laws, and the traditions of a people, or whether it should be carried out in deference to abstract principles, and arbitrary and general doctrines. (Disraeli's Edinburgh Speech, 1867)

Disraeli had believed that conservatism and democracy were natural allies and with marked political skill had put that belief into successful political effect. Salisbury, in whose temperament fear predominated over hope, took the opposite view. (Quinton, 1978, p. 87)

We are often told that conservatism is essentially ideology-free and that the Conservative Party is a common-sense party, which is pragmatic rather than philosophical. We should not take that defence too seriously. It often means no more than a preference for the status quo, which is just as much an ideological position as is a desire to change or reform institutions. The Conservative tends to look back to a golden age ('a better yesterday') whereas left-wing politicians look forward to a better future. Conservatives tend to condemn the latter as utopianism, whilst describing their own reluctance to embrace idealistic visions as pragmatism or common sense.

The Traditional Tory Mind

It may be helpful to begin by looking at some of those Conservatives who have been prepared to discuss conservative philosophy in ideological terms. Roger Scruton, a well-known English right-wing polemicist, prefers to avoid talking of conservative philosophy, describing his book *The Meaning of Conservatism* (1980) as dogmatics or a defence of a system of beliefs. Another apologist for conservatism, the American, Robert Nisbet (1986) also uses the term dogmatics. Scruton and Nisbet share a basic conservative belief that society has developed gradually over many generations, with a number of institutions acquiring useful functions. They suggest that so delicate is the balance of interests that has grown up over the years that it is extremely dangerous to try to change institutions. The more radical the change, the greater the risk. In this respect conservatism in politics has much in common with functionalism in sociology: society is an organic whole; change is always hazardous.

Later I shall have to return to Scruton, who has done much to define conservatism, not only in his books, but also as a leading member of the Conservative Philosophy Group (CPG). (Mrs Thatcher was a frequent attender of CPG meetings in its heyday.) Scruton has also written about conservative views on education to which I shall return in section 2. But first I want to go back to earlier centuries in order to see what motivated others who have been labelled, or who have labelled themselves, conservative. It will also be necessary to make a distinction between conservatism and the activities, even official policies, of the Conservative Party. It is usually accepted that the first requirement of a political party is to win the next election and for that doctrinal sacrifices may have to be made. But it is useful to spell out orthodoxy before considering deviations or heresies.

Edmund Burke (1729–97) is often quoted as an originator of much conservative thought, although he was, in the language of his day, a Whig rather than a Tory. (The word 'conservative' was not applied to political groups until about 1830.) Burke's *Reflections on the Recent Revolution in France* (1790) is still regarded as a classic expression of some basic conservative political values. In condemning the French Revolution, Burke explained why not only revolution but also radical reform is evil. He saw social continuity as essential for a society if the delicate balance of freedom and order were to be preserved; in advocating freedom, however, he was not preaching 'individualism' (a liberal doctrine) — human beings are essentially social animals and the customs of groups, including nations, must be revered. One of the social customs to be so respected was private property, which Burke and others have seen as a great force for order and stability.

Burke was particularly contemptuous of the abstract notion of 'natural rights' which had led the revolutionaries in France on to dangerous egalitarian (democratic) ideas about levelling out social class differences and eliminating privilege. He was equally contemptuous of the belief that Rousseau and his followers placed in the supremacy of human reason. Burke's view was that human beings were fallible and that the individual's 'Private stock of reason' was in constant need of guidance and restraint which would be provided from 'the general bank and capital of nations and ages'; naked reason had to be supplemented by authority and 'prejudice' (in the sense of preconceived social conventions which might or might not appear to be rational). Burke also believed that human beings were naturally religious and needed religion in order to avoid the calamitous mistakes typified by the French Revolution. For Burke the aristocracy embodied the 'Divine Will' as well as reason;ꞌ to revolt against the aristocracy was blasphemous as well as ignorant and irrational.

Benjamin Disraeli (1804–81) is often credited with setting out, a generation later, some of the policy guidelines of the Conservative Party. Robert Blake's book *The Conservative Party from Peel to Thatcher* (1985) acknowledges the claim that Disraeli was the founder of modern Conservatism, not only from the point of view of Party organization, but also in terms of ideas. 'It cannot be wholly accidental or erroneous that so many modern Conservatives look back on Disraeli as their prophet, high priest and philosopher rolled into one' (Blake, 1985, p. 3). Blake also makes a distinction between the ideologists of conservatism (like Burke) and of Toryism (like Coleridge): Conservatives defend the existing order; Tories, more romantically, 'look behind the institutions of their own generation to the spirit of the nation which gave them life' (p. 6). Later it will be clear that some aspects of Toryism are still alive in the Party, but generally I will use Tory and Conservative as synonyms. There is one important aspect of the Tory Mind which I will not attempt to deal with — the religious strand which was originally very important but by 1979 had ceased to be significant. It was no longer sensible to refer to the Church of England as the Conservative Party at prayer, although some Conservative politicians (including Margaret Thatcher) occasionally exploited the link. But more frequently she found herself embarrassed by a Church of England with 'socialist' ideas about compassion for the poor.

Disraeli was not only a successful politician but also a novelist. In both roles he contributed to conservative thinking: his 'One Nation' rhetoric was a partly successful attempt to gain working-class votes by stressing the identity of interests of different groups in society despite differences in wealth, income and life-style. Quinton (1978) in his classic text on conservatism suggests that Disraeli's main contribution to political theory was his short treatise *Vindication of the English Constitution*

(1835), which Quinton clearly does not rate very highly as a defence of tradition against utilitarian rationalism. Disraeli praises the English constitution as a product of countless generations' experience. In his practical politics he was, however, by no means a rigid adherent to traditions: for example, he saw the need for government intervention in such matters as factory legislation (to make conditions more like those he believed to exist between agricultural workers and their gentlemen masters). Such legislation has been seen as a step towards the welfare state.

Blake (1985) stresses the continuity of conservative attitudes from the mid-nineteenth century to the twentieth:

> The person who was a conservative . . . in Peel's day, his outlook, prejudices and passions, would have been quite recognisable to his counterpart who voted for Winston Churchill in the 1950s. There was a similar belief that Britain, especially England, was usually in the right. There was a similar faith in the value of diversity, of independent institutions, of the rights of property; a similar distrust of centralising officialdom, of the efficacy of government (except in the preservation of order and national defence), of Utopian panaceas and of 'doctrinaire' intellectuals; a similar dislike of abstract ideas, high philosophical principles and sweeping generalisations . . . A similar scepticism about human nature; a similar belief in original sin, and in the limitations of political and social amelioration; a similar scepticism about the notion of equality. (p. 359)

This may seem to be a curious list of qualities — unless we remember that Blake intended them as a mixture of 'outlook, prejudices and passions'. Even so, it is not entirely satisfactory, but will serve as a beginning.

Scruton's summary of conservative beliefs takes us a little further. It is spelt out in two books (1980, 1982) as well as in various issues of the Salisbury Review. Scruton (1982) talks of three aspects of conservatism: an attitude to society, an ideal of government and a political practice, all three of which are informed by, but not reducible to, scepticism. Conservatives should be sceptical particularly towards proposals for radical change, utopian theories, and liberal and socialist doctrines of human nature. Blake's list of attitudes, as well as Nisbet's suggestions, may be regrouped under Scruton's three headings (albeit with much overlap). I will try to summarize these views without distortion:

1 Attitude to society

1.1 A belief that Britain is usually in the right. This is more than crude patriotism, although at its worst it may become xenophobic; ideally it is a justifiable pride in national character. Baldwin (1938), for example, said 'I have always firmly held that there is no race with more ability latent than our own, or with a higher aptitude for mechanical genius' (p. 157). Churchill, and others, have believed that Britain was 'chosen' as a civilizing influence on the world.

1.2 A preference for diversity rather than uniformity or equality. This includes respect for rank (usually including the monarchy) and although there is a recent tendency to deny the existence of class, conservatives tend to be very class conscious — a characteristic which may border on snobbishness. This kind of 'pluralism' may involve segregation, partly because liberty is more important than equality. (We will see that this attachment to class is connected with conservative views on selection in education.)

1.3 Conservatives value independent institutions (rather than centralized controlling structures). An important function of society is to restrain man's passions and preserve order: for this purpose society must have authority and power, but power is better if widely distributed. We shall see that on this factor, some traditional Conservatives were disturbed at Margaret Thatcher's 'strong state' becoming too centralized.

2 Ideal of government

2.1 One main function of government is to preserve the status quo as far as possible. Falkland in the seventeenth century said 'When it is not necessary to change, it is necessary not to change.' This precept has often been repeated in more recent years. There is a distrust of centralized officials who may be tempted to make changes in the name of efficiency. Limited, but not minimal, government is preferred, the priorities being law and order, and national defence.

2.2 A major function of government is the preservation of property rights: property is more important than persons (although Baldwin sometimes doubted this). Taxation is a necessary evil but should be kept to a minimum and not used to redistribute wealth or property.

2.3 Tradition is preferable to contract, including the unnecessary contract of a written constitution. Tradition has a super-rational quality: *tradere* meant handing on something sacred. Looking back is better than trying to look forward: history is an account of decline not of progress (which was the Whig interpretation of history). An important Tory tradition was that rank and wealth were privileges which should be accompanied by responsibilities and duties — Baldwin was insistent on this.

3 Political practice

3.1 Political practice is guided not only by scepticism (of Liberal or socialist abstract ideals), but by pragmatism. There is a dislike of theories, or utopian planning, of abstract ideas and generalizations, and of intellectuals. It is worth noting Lord Salisbury's comment about Iain Macleod — 'too clever by half'. And Baldwin was not alone in thinking that 'intelligentsia was a very ugly name for a very ugly thing'. The Conservative Party is the Party of common sense: 'The British people have always been sceptical of starry-eyed idealists, and with good reason' (Francis Pym, 1984).

3.2 The dislike of utopian ideas is connected with a pessimistic view of human nature, sometimes taking the form of a belief in original sin or natural evil (Hobbes).

3.3 Prejudices (in the Edmund Burke sense of preconceptions) are 'natural'; even Conservative intellectuals like Oakeshott were suspicious of rationalism or a belief in total rationality. One interesting preconception is social class (which is, of course, an important factor in educational opportunity): Dennis Kavanagh (1987) tells us that in 1960 Macmillan wrote to a party official: 'Who are the middle classes? What do they want? How can we give it to them?' Many Conservatives, including Margaret Thatcher deny the existence of class whilst retaining a prejudice against lower-class behaviour: for example, Alan Clark (1993) betrayed his obsession with class when he said that his driver was typical of his class in losing his nerve so quickly when faced with difficulties; or, in a very different category, when he quoted with approval Jopling's criticism of Heseltine as one who 'had to buy all his own furniture' (p. 162). Clark was so obsessed with the idea of class that he agreed with those in the Conservative Party who believed that Margaret Thatcher was so good that she could not possibly have been a grocer's daughter, and built up a myth about her noble parentage.

An interesting insight into the British class structure occurs in Churchill and Mitchell (1974) which is a collection of Lady Randolph Churchill's correspondence. One chapter is about a famous divorce case involving Blandford, the future Duke of Marlborough.

> It is very difficult for us, a hundred years later, with divorce made easier year by year, to understand the horror its very mention sent through the upper classes in the 1870s. An anonymous French diplomat wrote that the dominating idea of English society

was not the cultivation of virtue, but the prevention of scandal, and he explained it as due to 'the extreme sensitiveness of the ladies and gentlemen prominent in London society to the public opinion of their inferiors'. But why were they so sensitive? Surely because they were fully aware that they belonged to an incredibly privileged class, and ever since the French Revolution privileged classes had looked anxiously over their shoulders. The only justification for their privileges was that they did, and were seen to do, their social duty; and that was to lead the nation not only politically but morally. Unfortunately, official Victorian morality, established by the Queen herself, and followed, at least in theory, by the respectable middle class, bore no relation whatever to upper class practice. Hence hypocrisy and cant now seem to be the chief characteristics of the period. (pp. 86–7)

This attempt to review traditional conservative attitudes and beliefs may be straining Scruton's framework too much. I must take the blame for that. For an alternative overview Quinton (1978) has a neater, more elegant classification of conservative principles (all of which, he claims, are derived from a basic belief in man's intellectual imperfection — which Quinton traces back to writers much earlier than Burke). The three principles are: traditionalism, organicism and scepticism. Traditionalism is expressed as reverence for established customs and institutions (and a corresponding hostility to sudden, precipitate change). Organicism takes a society to be:

a unitary, natural growth, an organised, living whole, not a mechanical aggregate. It is not composed of bare abstract individuals but of social beings, related to one another within a texture of inherited customs and institutions which endow them with their specific social nature. The institutions of society are thus not external, disposable devices, of interest to men only by reason of the individual purposes they serve; they are, rather, constitutive of the social identity of men. (Quinton, 1978, p. 16)

Scepticism is the belief that political wisdom is to be found not in the theoretical speculations of isolated thinkers, but 'in the historically accumulated experience of the community as a whole . . . in the deposit of traditional customs and institutions' (p. 17).

What all Conservatives have in common is a tendency to look back rather than forward for their social inspiration. Yesterday is likely to be better than the vision of tomorrow. They are concerned to preserve as much of the status quo as possible: change will probably — directly or indirectly — involve some loss of privilege for the class they belong to or aspire to.

Given that basic similarity there are several dimensions on which Conservatives will differ. One is the intensity of dislike for the modern world — ranging from the complete hatred of some modern values and behaviour in Evelyn Waugh's novels, to a milder exasperation and contempt in Alan Clark's diaries, and finally to a modest determination to cling to the most important aspects of a traditional way of life in R. A. Butler and Francis Pym. According to McKibbin (1990), Baldwin's Toryism proceeded from profound anxiety. His starting point was a belief that 'the times are new and strange and extraordinarily difficult'. The Great War had destroyed old certainties, disciplines, landmarks and practices, and Baldwin saw socialism as a threat to the traditional way of life.

A second dimension is the strategy adopted to preserve the status quo: democratic in the tradition of Disraeli's One Nation or demagogic — giving the people some of what they want as part of a package which may even turn the clock back. In other words, a genuine concern to make the best of democracy or a determination to subvert it (Scruton, for example, is occasionally openly contemptuous of democratic ideals).

I have outlined some of the features of the Tory Mind as well as some of the deep-rooted differences of type within that category; nearer the surface there are many differences of more or less importance according to the time — dislike of Europe or America, taxes, trade unions, social services, bureaucrats, planners, and so on.

If there is a coherent or semi-coherent set of political beliefs in conservatism, it may not always be easy to find such coherence in the statements of politicians or in Party manifestos. This is not only because the dogmatics sometimes yield to expediency, but also because policies are from time to time distorted by non-conservative dogmatics. But one of the themes of this book is that there is something which might be described as 'the Tory Mind' — with two qualifications. The first is that within the category there are degrees of intensity; the second is that norms change, to some extent, over time and are sometimes contaminated by non-Tory dogmatics such as the neo-liberal free market. Such a change was clearly taking place in the 1970s and it can be conveniently summarized as 'Thatcherism' — although, as we shall see in chapter 3, the influence of one individual should not be exaggerated. There was a tougher, anti-consensus stance being adopted by a new generation of Conservatives, some of them moving away from traditional

Tory paternalism towards neo-liberal economic and social attitudes — opposition to Keynesian policies and to the welfare state. It is not sensible to try to reduce these differences to a single dimension (from left to right or from wet to dry): it might be more appropriate to try to analyze a variety of factors around the dominant traditionalism outlined by Quinton and others.

The Tory Mind and Education

Before going into details of such ideological tensions — perhaps contradictions — we need to ask whether within conservative dogmatics there is a view of education. Some conservative politicians have, it seems, given little thought to the subject. Disraeli and many other Tory leaders have said little about education, apart from such splendid rhetoric as 'Upon the education of the people the fate of this country depends.' Others, less optimistic — or perhaps more frank — were doubtful about educating the lower orders: 'The future Tory Prime Minister, Lord Salisbury, characterised the attempt to establish systematic primary education in Britain as "pumping learning into louts"' (Ross, 1983, p. 30). When Baldwin spoke of education he did not usually have in mind formal education in schools and universities. His collected speeches (Baldwin, 1938) include three on education: 'Self-Education', 'Political Education' and 'Teachers and Taught' (all three given in 1923–4). They tell us more about Baldwin's attitude to life in general than his vision for a better education service:

> I think you learn — not by being taught, but by that instinct which comes with wider knowledge — you learn a healthy distrust of rhetoric. If there is any class to be regarded with suspicion in a democracy it is the rhetoritician — the man who plays on half-educated people with fallacies which they are incapable of detecting. More than one democracy has been wrecked by that. (p. 167)

Harold Macmillan was, according to his biographer, Alistair Horne (1989), not interested in education, but happily supported his modernizing, pluralist Minister of Education, David Eccles. Whitelaw (1989) in his *Memoirs* does not discuss education, Tory education policies or the views of any Education Secretary. Perhaps predictably, Alan Clark, whose diaries covered the years 1983–91, did not even mention the Education Reform Act of 1988; the only reference to education was a passing sneer at new university professors of such subjects as 'Industrial Trade' (p. 306).

In general, however, Conservatives tend to take for granted that society is, and should be, divided hierarchically into ranks or classes, and that the Platonic view of different kinds of educational training for different levels in society is part of the natural order. R. A. Butler in his autobiography *The Art of the Possible* (1971) describes his interviews with Churchill which clearly betrayed that attitude. Butler himself was interested in education and saw the need for improved schooling for all. But he was careful in the 1944 Education Act not to disturb the private system. He said that 'The first class carriage had been shunted onto an immense siding' (p. 121). Even in 1994 all the Cabinet and most Conservative MPs use private schools for their own children.

Churchill felt that a public system of education was necessary in a modern society, but running it was a low-status job. He thought Butler could do no harm at the Board of Education. Butler considered that Churchill's interest in education was 'slight, intermittent and decidedly idiosyncratic' (p. 109). Churchill did touch on the subject of education in one of his famous BBC speeches towards the end of the war: it was, according to Butler, derived from Disraeli's view that a nation rules either by force or by tradition:

> His theme was that we must adhere to our traditions, but that we must move from the class basis of our politics, economics and education to a national standard. There were some sharp words about idle people whether at the top or the bottom, some very pungent remarks about the old school tie (the time for which, he said, was past), and a definite assertion that the school leaving-age must be raised to 16. He remarked that his daughter Mary had told him he must say 16, 'because it had been promised', and that he agreed with her as this would keep people off the labour market . . . (p. 113)

At that time (during World War II) there was little open disagreement about education in the Conservative Party — Butler, Churchill and their colleagues assumed that there needed to be schools for the majority but that they would be different from the elite public schools. The main dispute was how good schools for the masses ought to be and how much could be afforded in practice. The difference between the two school systems was not simply a question of expense or quality, it was a question of function. In the nineteenth century independent schools were intended to produce the future leaders of society — at home or in the Empire — whereas state schools would produce workers of various kinds. Since 1902 grammar schools had provided a 'ladder of opportunity' for the academically able, a few of whom might even join the ranks of the true leaders. It was important to preserve diversity. The 1944 Act and secondary education for all was welcomed by all Parties — but in retrospect it is easy to see that it was interpreted differently by the Conservative and Labour Parties.

How good the state system needed to be would, I suggest, eventually become one of the issues dividing conservatives into traditionalists and modernizers, or in my own terms, minimalists and pluralists (see below).

A main purpose of education of any kind for the conservatives has always been character-building. But different kinds of character are needed for different positions in the social hierarchy: leadership for some — the Christian gentleman ideal — and training for patriotic, obedient subjects of the Queen in elementary schools: Churchill urged Butler in 1941 to 'tell the children that Wolfe won Quebec' (Butler, 1971, p. 91).

We need to see the development of state education (and changing conservative attitudes to education) in the context of social, economic and political change in the nineteenth and twentieth centuries. Robert Lowe (1867) did not quite say 'We must educate our masters', but he was quite clear that an important function of elementary schools was to ensure the continued subservience of the lower orders. Elementary schools had always been concerned with good order, obedience and habits of industry; after the 1867 Act, which extended the franchise to more of the working class, elementary schools needed to be sufficiently improved to ensure correct voting behaviour. The 1870 Elementary Education Act soon followed.

This may appear to be an unfair picture of the mid-nineteenth century education system, but there is ample evidence to show that this was very largely the situation at least until the 1944 Act when there was a significant shift — free secondary education for all — which intensified differences of views about the organization of state schooling (especially the question of selection), as well as the costs of the education service. We shall see that a debate about education developed within the Conservative Party during the 1950s and 1960s, reaching a climax with the beginning of Thatcherism in the 1970s. Meanwhile, is it possible to map out a coherent set of Conservative education values?

It may be useful at this point to return to the views of a Conservative who has studied conservatism and theorized about conservative education. Roger Scruton (1980) has stressed the importance of the institutions of education:

> through which politicians have rightly perceived that a major battle for the soul of society must be fought, some moved by a sense that education has certain inherent standards, without which it imparts nothing to the value of human life, others moved by the knowledge that it also confers privileges which they demand to be more widely distributed. Through the smoke of this quarrel we discern the vital distinction between education as means and education as end. (p. 147)

Scruton goes on to make the point that Conservatives are unlikely to be worried by the probability that some kinds of education confer privileges; he is very critical of 'egalitarians' who wish to abolish such privileges not only because these attempts in themselves are misguided, but also because they run the risk of destroying the very institution they intend to improve. This is a common Tory point of view: institutions have developed into their present form over many generations; it is dangerous to try to change them; you must put up with a few features that you might not like.

Scruton represents only one aspect of Conservative thinking — those who argue for education for its own sake (which is, of course, a view shared by many outside conservative ranks). Scruton believes that, although the value of rationality should not be exaggerated, education is essentially a rational process in which the child is rationally engaged — exercising his own understanding. This is quite different from training or indoctrination.

Scruton sees as one of the problems of state education the fact that since schooling is compulsory 'it becomes impossible to construe the teacher's authority as acquired by parental delegation'. Scruton, whilst criticizing some of the Thatcherite education policies (for example, vocationalism) is in favour of encouraging parental choice. As we shall see, from the 1960s onwards, 'parental choice' has become a central plank of Conservative education policy, not necessarily for Scruton's reason but also because the Conservatives became increasingly captivated by the ideology of 'the market'.

To pursue that issue now would be to anticipate later chapters. What I am trying to do at this stage is simply to outline some basic conservative principles about education. I have already suggested that Scruton represents the thinking of those whose main belief is in 'education for its own sake' (the group Raymond Williams (1961) referred to as 'old humanists'). According to Scruton's exposition of this view, education needs no justification, but it will possess certain characteristics. Apart from being a rational activity, education will also foster the kinds of knowledge, understanding and beliefs that work to preserve those aspects of society thought to be most worthwhile; anything which encourages change will not be educational.

In the nineteenth century the classics — Greek and Latin literature, history and some philosophy — were a perfect diet for the future leaders of society; for the others, religious instruction, literacy and numeracy were essential plus the kind of history, geography and English literature which would foster loyalty to Queen, country and Empire. And it worked: during World War I, working-class products of elementary schools were used as loyal cannon-fodder by their social superiors.

By the twentieth century the independent school curriculum had to change: the classics remained but were no longer dominant; they were partly replaced by more mathematics and science as well as English history and literature to provide the cultural heritage needed to encourage the preservation of as much of the social status quo as possible. The secondary grammar schools made possible by the 1902 Education Act were required by the 1904 Secondary Regulations to follow that example with a curriculum which was deliberately different from what was legally provided in elementary schools. The scholarship system ensured that the most academic working-class children would be 'creamed off' to support the leaders of society educated in the public schools (in other words independent schools).

The system worked well. The conventional wisdom within the Conservative Party by the beginning of the twentieth century was that it was worth paying public money in this way, partly to ensure that the right kind of cultural heritage was transmitted to the young. The best independent schools would always provide something extra.

There was, however, a conservative view which differed from the 'cultural heritage' view. The alternative ideology saw servicing the labour market as the major purpose of education. Some have referred to this group as the 'vocational trainers' or 'industrial trainers' (Williams, 1961). They saw the need to expand the numbers of clerks and civil servants. By the end of the nineteenth century, and even more so by the end of World War I, there was a third group, including some Conservatives: those who felt that the extension of the franchise had to be matched by a further extension of educational provision. This argument (combined with the need for better trained manpower) eventually won the day during World War II when the reform of education was discussed in parallel with the Beveridge proposals for a post-war welfare state, but that does not necessarily mean that all Conservatives were completely convinced.

Much of this story is familiar. What I would wish to focus on, however, is that just as Robert Blake (1985) could say that in general conservative attitudes remained the same throughout the nineteenth and twentieth centuries, so we must also find out whether the nineteenth-century attitudes on education are still in existence, possibly in modified forms. What I want to do in the chapters which follow is to explore the ideological thinking behind these varieties of conservatism. We need to analyze what T. S. Eliot (1955) described as the 'pre-political' — the 'stratum down to which any sound political thinking must push its roots and from which it must derive nourishment'.

Another strand or theme of this book is that despite the enduring qualities of conservatism, the centre of gravity changes over time. Until recently it was assumed by many that the changes were unidirectional (the ratchet effect that Keith Joseph and Margaret Thatcher condemned as creeping socialism; Evelyn Waugh also complained that no Con-servative government had ever turned the clock back). It may be useful to summarize this evolution of ideas under three phases of Conservat-ive ideology: from private education in the early nineteenth century, to minimalism by the end of the nineteenth century, and then to pluralism at the end of World War II. (There is a fourth stage — comprehensive planning — which is, I suggest, not encompassed by the Tory Mind).

The Age of Private Education

During the early years of the nineteenth century the majority of politic-ians in England believed that education was essentially a private matter and that the state should not get involved — schools for the masses could be left for the churches to organize. This principle was broken in 1833 when a small sum of money was voted by Parliament to sub-sidize the two voluntary (religious) bodies involved in elementary edu-cation; during this period the state was involved in financing schools but not in owning or managing them, although from 1839 inspectors were appointed to make sure that state money was correctly spent. Many educationists believed that the argument had been finally settled — that is, in a modern society it would always be necessary for the state to be involved in education. But there have always been some Tories who still believe that it was a mistake for the state to be in-volved: I refer to such Conservatives as the 'Privatizers'.

A Minimalist System for the Masses

It was not until the 1870 Education Act that a second stage began: the Act established a state system of elementary schools, filling the gaps in the voluntary system; but the schools were not intended to rival what was provided for fee-paying middle-class children. It was a *minimalist* system. In the much quoted words of H. G. Wells it was:

> not an Act for a common universal education, it was an Act to educate the lower classes for employment on lower class lines, and with specially trained, inferior teachers. (*Experiment in Auto-biography*, 1934, p. 93)

The 1870 Act was supplemented in 1902 by the Balfour Act (named after the Conservative Prime Minister) which permitted local authorities (counties) to set up secondary schools generally modelled on the existing private grammar schools. But this was not intended to be a universal provision; it was merely a 'ladder of opportunity' intended to *select* a tiny minority of able lower-class children and assist them to be educated out of their class. It was still a minimalist system, but even so some Conservatives — the Privatizers — were reluctant to support it.

Pluralism

The minimalist view prevailed within the Conservative Party until World War II when, as we have seen, Butler was entrusted with the task of limited education reform: the 1944 Act, which will be discussed in chapter 2, was the beginning of a third period which I refer to as *pluralist*. The 1944 Act was passed during the period of planning for a better post-war world and had the support of most Conservatives. This was partly because the major principle of the Act, 'secondary education for all', meant different things to different politicians. For some Conservatives the Act was a continuation of minimalism: only a few would have a real secondary education — in a grammar school — the others would be selected out for inferior training in technical and modern schools; but for other Conservatives, probably a minority, the Act meant three different kinds of school for different kinds of 'ability' with 'parity of prestige' — an essentially pluralist notion.

Comprehensive Planners

Very few Conservatives, if any, interpreted the 1944 Act in terms of education as a 'broad highway' or a system which would provide the same standard of education for all young people — this was regarded by Conservatives as a socialist idea. I refer to the 'broad highway' view as the vision of the 'comprehensive planners' and it is possible that it is simply incompatible with Conservative dogmatics.

Conservatives range from those who are frankly contemptuous of democratic views about education for all, to those who, whilst supporting some aspects of quality education for everyone, stop short at accepting the logic of a fully non-selective system. We will find several examples of Conservatives of that kind in the following chapters. We will also find that some Conservatives are still 'privatizers' or 'minimalists' at heart — looking back to the nineteenth century, rather than accepting the pluralist logic of the 1944 Act or looking forward to a society which needs much higher standards of education for all. This revival of nineteenth century attitudes in education can also be identified, to some extent, with the move to Thatcherism from 1975 onwards. There was a departure from the more traditional, paternalistic community values of Butler, Eccles and Boyle towards individualistic views about parental choice, selective schools and vouchers. Clyde Chitty (1989) has documented the marked difference between the first three Black Papers (Cox and Dyson 1969a, 1969b, 1970) and the final two (Cox and Boyson 1975 and 1977). The right-wing offensive began; the ratchet was reversed.

Chapter 2

From Consensus to Conflict 1944–79

Do those who say that government expenditure could be drastically reduced propose a reversal of policy in education, or a cut in the cost of pensions? Or are we to hold up work on the roads? Perhaps I can answer by saying that in each of these spheres we have to do all we can to meet imperative needs — in the case of education, of a rising school population, in the case of the old of an increased number of retired persons, and in the case of the roads, with a programme which I cannot increase but which is already insufficient to deal with the needs of the country. (R. A. Butler presenting Autumn Budget, 1955)

A year later Edward Boyle decided to retire from politics. This was a great blow to the Party. Edward was very much on the liberal wing, with such a magnificent intellect that even those who detested his views admired him. There is a nasty element in every party, and for some politicians the time comes when they get so sickened by the constant infighting that they either explode or withdraw. But the loss of Edward Boyle was more than that of one man: it was a tilt to the right, because Margaret Thatcher, who had joined the Shadow Cabinet as Power spokesman in 1967 and had become Transport spokesman in 1968, now became Education spokesman. (Jim Prior, 1986, p. 53)

Chapter 1 was concerned with some enduring features of Conservative ideology. Much was made of the fact that the characteristics that shaped Disraeli's policies were still recognizable to those who voted Conservative in the 1980s. But, ideologies also change to some extent. One of the questions we have to address, looking at the post-war years, is how the 1944 Act may have brought about changes in ideology. And since 1944 there have been other changes: the attitudes of Conservative politicians in opposition (1945–51); the developing education policies in the thirteen years of Conservative rule (1951–64); in opposition again at a time of economic crises (1964–70); and the failure of consensus policies under Ted Heath. Or did ideology change as a result of other factors — economic, social and political — during those years?

The main method I shall employ to trace Tory thinking on education will be to look at what Conservative Education Ministers (and a few others) have said about education. It will also be relevant to analyze what has been said about them. For some of that period the education debate was mainly between Conservative minimalists and pluralists (that is, between those who wanted a low-cost, limited education service and those who wanted good quality — but different — education for all). But as we shall see, a reaction began to set in during the late 1960s, when the views of Privatizers became important once again.

The 1944 Education Act and R. A. Butler

I have deliberately avoided giving this Act the title of 'The Butler Act', because that is to beg a big question. It may indeed be useful, in examining Butler's part in the development of Conservative education policy, to see how well he fits into the description of the Tory Mind set out in chapter 1.

We are fortunate that not only did Rab provide us with his own version of reality in his memoirs (Butler, 1971 and 1982), but also that those versions have been submitted to critical scrutiny in Anthony Howard's (1987) official biography, whose interpretation on some matters has been challenged, for example by Heaton and Goodfellow (1987). On some fundamentals, however, there appears to be agreement. It seems, for example, that Rab never considered joining any other political party — the Conservative Party was his natural home. Why? It seems that his family had been Conservatives for several generations, and he did not feel out of place in their ranks at university or after. Moreover, he betrays certain important class loyalties (despite an occasional tendency to irreverence), and his own personality or temperament was, for whatever reason, decidedly conservative. It may not be too fanciful to suggest that the main difference between Butler and his Labour opponent Gaitskell was class: not their own social class status, which was very similar (their fathers were both upper-middle-class public servants), nor their education (both went to elite public schools), but their attitudes to class.

Gaitskell saw class as an obstacle to social justice in society — including educational opportunities — and felt guilty about the privileges that his own class background had given him. Butler, on the other hand, saw class and property as aspects of a good, stable society;

privileges could be enjoyed but should also be put to good use — for the community as a whole as well as for individual benefit. But even with a Conservative as moderate as Butler, there is a tendency to exaggerate the significance of class at the personal level, whilst underestimating its social power. In his chapter on Chips Channon, Butler (1982) showed himself to be extremely sensitive about questions of personal social status:

> 'Lunched alone with Rab (off pork) at Smith Square' is another earlier entry. Chips manages to make it sound as though my modest housekeeper's unpretentious choice of pork demonstrated a curious difference between us. One might almost say it was a difference in class, from his comments. One might almost say that he felt himself to be an aristocrat from Chicago, whilst I was a Minister risen from the ranks. In fact my ancestors, the Butlers of Ireland, had been hereditary cup-bearers and holders of high office for generations, not to mention that my grandfather and father had been academics of distinction. (p. 53)

Gaitskell, whatever his other faults might have been, could never have written anything like that.

Butler could admire those from working-class origins, for example, Ernie Bevin (Butler, 1982), but he admired him as an outsider — in the way he suggests Lord Halifax admired Gandhi. They were to be respected for their sincerity as opponents, but if it was necessary for them to win a few battles, it was important to make sure that the major features of the social fabric were not disturbed. Containing the Indian problem had something in common with keeping the lower orders under control in England. A belief in class, whether conscious or not, is, I suggest, a powerful support for the principle and practice of selection within the education system.

Rab was much more interested in education than most of his contemporaries in the Party. There was a Butler family tradition of being schoolmasters and Oxbridge dons, and Butler whilst still at Cambridge considered, but soon dismissed, the possibility of schoolmastering. The reason he gave (in a letter to his father) may be significant:

> You know how keen I am on the Diplomatic . . . I definitely do not want to do schoolmastering, my talents are not in that line. They are in mixing with great and interesting people and seeing life and getting the best out of it. I am fired by national as well

as personal temperament and would be happiest in the rever-
beration and interclash of nations. (Howard, p. 20)

The Diplomatic Service would have strained the Butler family resources and Rab might have been obliged to have settled for a career
as a Cambridge don, but for a fortunate marriage to an heiress —
Sydney Courtauld — which provided him with ample independent
means for the rest of his life. From that point on there was no doubt
about his career — he gave up his Fellowship and became a Conservative MP.

As an MP he was conventional, disagreeing openly with other young
Conservatives such as Harold Macmillan who advocated radical change
on a number of social issues. Butler was a Party man, even to the point
of supporting — as a junior minister — the Chamberlain/Halifax line
on appeasing Hitler, which was a policy he seems to have genuinely
believed in. Like many others at that time, he felt that a 'democracy' like
Britain could and should coexist peacefully with totalitarian regimes.
He survived the fall of Chamberlain without completely renouncing his
views about appeasing Hitler. He got on well with Churchill, although
privately he referred to him as a 'half-breed American' (Howard, p. 92).
In 1941 he accepted Churchill's offer of promotion to the post of President of the Board of Education without undue hesitation.

At this point the story is open to more than one interpretation.
How much of the 1944 Act is his own work? Kevin Jefferys (1984)
examined precisely this question and eventually agreed with Peter
Gosden (1976) that the major credit for the content of the Act should
have gone to the officials at the Board of Education. Wallace (1981)
also showed that the major decisions about what would be needed
after the war had been made before Butler became President of the
Board in 1941. Edward Boyle (1976) agreed with that view. What Butler
did — and did extremely well — was to provide the political authority
without which the ideas in the Green Paper would never have become
an Act. Jefferys is also interested in the extent to which the Act was
the result of cooperative work and pressures from the Labour Party.

As far as this chapter is concerned, however, the important question is the amount of support that Butler was prepared to give to crucial
aspects of reform previously proposed by civil servants. According to
Wallace, not only were all the main ideas in place before Butler arrived
at the Board, but they had to be defended against Butler's 'considerable
doubts' about such matters as free secondary schooling and the raising
of the school leaving age. Butler was eventually persuaded by his civil
servants to press ahead quietly (despite Churchill's veto on legislation

during the war). Butler supported the idea of different kinds of second-ary school for different kinds of ability, but was anxious that they should all be treated with equity (the doctrine later known as 'parity of esteem'). He felt that sooner or later selection had to be an inevitable part of the system even if in a rural area, for example, a comprehensive school might be regarded as a desirable solution.

What took a good deal of Butler's time was solving the problem of the dual system, especially providing for voluntary (religious) schools in a way which would not offend either the Church of England, or the Roman Catholic and non-Conformist groups. Churchill and Butler were sensitive to this political trap as were other senior Conservatives, but Butler managed this superbly. He also had to persuade the Treasury that education reforms would not cost too much too soon. There were plenty of possible excuses for delay, but eventually (November 1942) Chuter Ede, Butler's Labour Party Junior Minister, warned Butler that the Labour Party would cause trouble unless legislation was seen to be clearly on the way: Ede said that they feared the 1918 trick — keeping the Labour Party within the government until victory and then pushing them out to restore pre-war standards. Approval to draft a Bill was hastened by the 'belligerence' of Ernie Bevin (Jeffereys, p. 426). It is clear that getting any kind of Bill through was difficult, but Rab care-fully went out of his way to avoid offending Conservative opinion:

> In practice . . . he (Butler) was far more concerned with yielding to the views of the Conservative party. This had been evident from an early stage when it was decided not to tackle the prob-lems of the Public Schools in any legislation. Butler hoped that this question would 'lie quiet' under the consideration of the Fleming Committee, and he reassured the backbench 1922 Committee that the position of the Public Schools would be safeguarded after the war. (Jeffereys, p. 427, referring to the Butler Papers)

As legislation came closer, Butler gave in to Conservative pressure on retaining the selective Direct Grant Schools, and emphasized the divers-ity and variety of secondary schools in the White Paper (1943). Many Conservatives were also opposed to the abolition of fees in other sec-ondary schools; Butler persuaded them that it was an inevitable conse-quence of making secondary education compulsory. This ruse worked when the Bill was discussed in the Commons — but by then the Pres-ident felt the real danger might be that the Tories were getting bored by the whole thing. The Act was an achievement for Butler who was also pleased that he had safeguarded his Party's interests: 'Diversity and variety among the state schools, the place of religious instruction, and the autonomy of the Public Schools' (Jeffereys, p. 430).

Anthony Howard is particularly critical of Butler's failure to tackle the problem of public schools at a time when a real solution might have been possible. Chuter Ede on 4 February 1942 was summoned to Churchill and offered promotion (to the Ministry of War Transport). Ede refused and wrote an interesting account of the meeting:

> The P.M. was glad to know that the public schools were receiving our attention. He wanted 60–70 per cent of the places to be filled by bursaries — not by examination alone but on the recommendation of the counties and the great cities. 'We must reinforce the ruling-class' — though he disliked the word 'class'. We must not choose by the mere accident of birth and wealth, but by the accident — for it was equally accident — of ability. The great cities would be proud to search for able youths to send to Haileybury, to Harrow and to Eton. (Quoted in Howard, p. 119)

Churchill's proposal, had it been sincere, would have gone further than anything that Butler had in mind for integrating the public schools into the state system and far exceeded the proposals that eventually emerged from the Fleming Report (1945) which proved to be so unappealing as to be no basis for any post-war policy. Even so, the principle of selection would have been preserved and perhaps strengthened — Churchill's comments about the 'accident of ability' reveal his attitude to egalitarian policies.

Rab is often regarded as an exemplar of enlightened post-war Conservative attitudes. It will be interesting to examine how well he fits in to the model set out in chapter 1. Since Rab has so often been praised for his work in the field of education, it may be profitable to analyze his contribution to education reform in the light of what has already been stated about 'the Tory Mind'.

Rab fully acknowledged the need for a good state system. He was never one who wished to revert to a fully private set of schools. But was he a minimalist or a pluralist? On the evidence of his own writing (especially Butler, 1971) it might be tempting to regard him as a pluralist — one who believed in good quality education for all, whilst preserving different kinds of schooling for different kinds of children (including private schools for those who wanted them and could afford them). Howard (1987) describes Rab as a meritocrat and is critical of Rab on the public school issue:

It has to be conceded that Rab's handling of the public schools question represented the one real failure in his general strategy for educational reconstruction. The time was ripe, the public mood was propitious, the opportunity was there. And yet he contrived to throw it all away. Why? The cynical answer would, no doubt, be that as an ex-public schoolboy himself, a parent who sent his own three sons to Eton, and an Essex M.P. who dutifully sat on the governing body of one of the county's own public schools, Felsted, he lacked enthusiasm for the task in hand . . . (p. 122)

On other evidence it is clear that Butler, when he became Chancellor of the Exchequer in 1951, retreated from the responsibility of providing for 'parity of esteem' and questioned the need for the large sums of money being requested by the Minister of Education, Florence Horsburgh (Lawrence, 1992, p. 25).

In 1954, Richard Crossman wrote a profile for the New Statesman, 'The Ideologist of Inequality', in which he described Butler as a Platonist concerned to preserve a society 'controlled by an elite and within a framework of authority'. According to Crossman, the challenge facing conservatism was 'not to oppose public ownership or planning or the welfare state, but to use them . . . to maintain the differences of wealth and status which are essential to stability (quoted in Howard, p. 365). Exactly so, except that I would want to add education to the list of institutions that Butler (and other modernizing Conservatives) sought to use to 'maintain differences of wealth and status'. Howard also points out that Butler was much concerned with the possibility that capitalism might bring about its own downfall and he was, therefore, prepared to be a reluctant modernizer. Had Rab been more visionary (that is, less Tory) he could have solved the public school problem; in the event, he failed to do for education what Bevan later succeeded in doing for the National Health Service — bring the prestigious teaching hospitals into the state system. Butler probably could have, but clearly did not wish to risk failure or even controversy within the Conservative Party. A real opportunity was missed.

1951–64: Thirteen Wasted Years?

The Conservative Party were in opposition 1945–51, but were in office continuously from 1951 to 1964. During those thirteen years there were five Ministers of Education (the senior position was changed to

Secretary of State in 1964), two of them, Eccles and Hailsham, serving twice.

Florence Horsburgh

Florence Horsburgh, the first post-war Conservative Minister of Education (1951–54), need not delay us for long: Maurice Kogan (1978) sums up her career in education as 'a dreary and disliked Minister who was brought only late into the Cabinet, who never fought for and never received an adequate educational budget'. (p. 34). Edward Boyle (1976), normally a kindly observer, volunteered (in the context of the Teachers Superannuation Bill, 1954) that 'Miss Horsburgh, for all her experience, was never a master of lucid exposition' (p. 2) and later commented on her 'proven lack of Parliamentary capacity' (p. 3). In 1954 she was replaced by David Eccles.

David Eccles

Eccles is often spoken of as a modernizing Conservative education minister along with Butler and Boyle. Eccles had two periods in office: 1954–6 and 1959–62. His reputation rests partly on his ability to extract money from the Treasury and therefore enable Local Education Authorities (LEAs) to build and improve. But what of his ideas on education? In 1955 he told the National Union of Teachers' (NUT) Conference about his five working rules on secondary education:

1 A new range of 15–25 per cent for grammar plus technical school places.
2 New technical schools would be approved where there was a very strong case.
3 Modern schools would be encouraged to develop extended courses and to strengthen their links with grammar and technical schools, and with further education.
4 Transfers should be made as early as possible to put right glaring mistakes in the examination. Otherwise the time for transfers — and more should be arranged — should be at 15 or 16.
5 Comprehensive schools would be approved as an experiment when all the conditions were favourable and no damage was done to any existing schools. (Quoted in Gosden, 1983, p. 31)

This list would seem to express a desire for an efficient, meritocratic system rather than a new vision — Kogan (1978) sums it up as 'optimism and opportunism' (p. 34). Eccles is also credited by Kogan with being the first Minister to employ economic arguments in favour of increasing expenditure on education — the 'Education as investment' thesis which was powerful in the 1950s and 1960s, but was later to be questioned. We should also give credit to Eccles for his tremendous efforts to eliminate all-age schools — those schools that despite the 1944 Act were still organized on a 5–15 elementary school basis and in many cases resembled the pre-1944 school in ethos, organization and curriculum. Removing such schools represented a genuine move in the direction of secondary education for all. Eccles clearly saw this campaign as part of a drive for standards and quality. But Lawrence (1992, p. 26) sees him as a Tory romantic.

This was a judgment that I found strange until I had read Eccles' book *Life and Politics: A Moral Diagnosis* (1967) which is a collection of rather repetitive essays on the problems of the modern world and the need to go back to Christian solutions. He saw 'socialist' ideas on education, emphasizing equality, as an undesirable alternative to what he saw as a Christian model of a well-ordered society where all ranks understood their responsibilities and duties rather than their rights. In this context he betrayed a familiar Tory distrust of intellectual solutions involving planning:

> The Labour Party took it for granted that men would work more loyally and efficiently when the state replaced the private capitalist as the owner of mines and railways. The lesson is clear: before any big reform is introduced politicians must be able to count on the moral response required to make it a success. Failure to do this is the besetting weakness of intellectuals. They either do not know what men and women are really like, or do not care how they behave. When their ingenious plans go wrong, they become annoyed and demand the use of force; and, if they then get their way, before we realise it, we find ourselves, as Lord Radcliffe has said, 'Totalitarians by the back door'. (p. 31)

He also shares a typical Conservative attitude to class:

> In 1943 I was elected to serve in Parliament for the Chippenham division of Wiltshire. I had joined the Conservatives because they were against the class war and had a long record of trying to be a truly national party. Their breadth of outlook appeared

to be no accident but due to a better understanding of the strength and weakness of human nature than could be found in the other parties. (p. 41)

This view of class is, of course, connected with Conservative views on 'equality':

> We can give every man the vote, a pension and free medical treatment, but we cannot make him his neighbour's equal. Men are in fact staggeringly unequal, as everyone discovers in his home, in his school, his place of work, the income tax returns or the House of Commons . . . (p. 72–3)

Or again:

> If, then, the progressive equalisation of growing wealth will not produce a good standard of morals, what will? The true answer . . . was given by the 4th century writer Lactantius when he said that 'genuine equality depends upon the suppression of selfish pride and arrogance rather than any mechanical re-arrangement of material goods'. Character counts more than fair shares. To treat someone else as equal, to show him that you mind about him as a person, is more important than to hand him £5 of the taxpayers' money . . . (p. 132)

A comfortable status quo philosophy for someone with an income well above average. But he was on the side of the pluralists in the Party:

> Were we trying to produce . . . a small elite or were we trying rather to produce in everyone the virtues hitherto characteristic of the middle classes. The Minister favoured the latter view. (Eccles, 23 February 1955; quoted by Dean, 1992, p. 10)

Dean (1992) also shows that the thinking behind Eccles' motives for improving education may be features of the Tory Mind:

> a half-educated electorate is fodder for the class war and a menace to free institutions. Problems such as forestalling infla-tion, settling strikes and arbitrary restrictive practices will in the end only be solved by a better educated electorate. (Eccles to Eden 6 June 1955; quoted by Dean, 1992, p. 11).

We should not, however, forget that it was Eccles who saw the need for greater national efforts in terms of the curriculum and that it was his initiative which produced the Curriculum Study Group in 1962 which the *Times Educational Supplement* (TES) described as 'Eccles' most imaginative and far-reaching legacy' (quoted in Gosden, 1983, p. 77). Eccles wanted a broader curriculum — to produce better workers. Boyle (1976) also admired Eccles: 'I regard David Eccles as still by far the most under-rated figure who held office during the thirteen years of Conservative rule' (p. 20). That judgment may also tell us something about Boyle.

Quintin Hogg, Lord Hailsham

Quintin Hogg succeeded to his father's title of Viscount Hailsham in 1950, but gave up his title in 1963 in order to be a candidate for the post of Prime Minister when Macmillan resigned, but he became Lord Hailsham again in 1970 with a life peerage in order to become Lord Chancellor. He spent two brief periods in charge of education: January to September 1957 and April to October 1964. He confesses (1990) that this was not a position he had sought and he seems to have had little interest in it. Out of 463 pages of his autobiography only eight are devoted to the chapter on 'Minister of Education' and little of that is about education. He accused Shirley Williams of 'educational philistinism' and the Labour Party of 'fanatical egalitarianism'. Having aired his prejudices about the advantages of private education, competition and the awfulness of comprehensive schools, he concludes:

> My own view is and was that education is far too important an issue to be made the plaything of Party politics and that doctrinaire theories based on the preferability of one sort of structure rather than another have no objective reality at all, and ought to give way to an atmosphere of objective analysis, open-mindedness, variety and parental choice. (p. 306)

The book is interesting only for revealing what a senior Tory took for granted as common sense: separate (private) schools for the professional classes, the privileges they bestowed throughout life, that comprehensive schools could not work and that state schools were spiritual deserts. He contributed nothing to policy ideas during his two periods in office, but he was concerned about the low standards of some aspects of the service, and did his best to improve its organization and funding, seeing education as an investment for industrial survival (Dean, 1992). For the same reason, Hogg wanted more science in the curriculum, but during his time little was done to achieve it.

Geoffrey Lloyd

Geoffrey Lloyd also served for only a short time — 1957–59. His obituary in *The Times* (13 September 1984) claimed that he was the first man of a technological bent to occupy the post of Minister of Education and that he had done much to enhance the standing of technology. But Lawrence (1992) disagrees on the grounds that 'technology was still a long way from receiving academic approval in the schools'. (p. 28). Like many Conservative Ministers of Education, he had been to a Public School (Harrow) and possessed little or no knowledge of the state system. Apart from the technology claim dismissed by Lawrence, as far as I can discover, no one has suggested that he made any significant contribution to educational ideas or policies. But Dean (1992) says he used PR effectively to secure more funds for education, especially after the success of the Russian Sputnik. Lloyd was also impressed by some American ideas on education but, after his return from the USA, he was still intent on preventing the kind of sweeping comprehensivization common in the USA and supported by the Labour Party.

Sir Edward Boyle

Boyle merits a good deal of attention in our search for the Tory Mind on education for two reasons. First, he wrote extensively about education in the context of Conservative Party policies; second, he may be the best example of a Conservative who pushed rational pragmatism so far that many condemned him for ceasing to be a Conservative. I shall suggest, however, that this is not true: his views remained those of a Conservative despite the fact that they became so unpopular that he left politics in 1970 in order to become Vice-Chancellor of Leeds University. Kogan (1971) refers to him as a 'reluctant Conservative' (p. 20) and this is probably as good a description as any.

Edward Boyle had the perfect background for a Conservative Minister: inheriting a baronetcy and, like Hailsham, going to Eton and Christ Church, Oxford, where he was President of the Union. He entered Parliament in 1950, aged 27, as the MP for Handsworth, Birmingham, and retained this seat until 1970. In 1956 when he was a Junior

Treasury Minister, he resigned in protest against the Conservative Suez adventure. But he was soon forgiven and in 1957 Macmillan offered him the junior post in education under Hailsham. He remained in the Ministry of Education until 1959 when he was promoted to be Financial Secretary to the Treasury, remaining there until becoming Minister of Education in 1962. In 1964 this Ministry was combined with Science to form the Department of Education and Science (DES); Boyle remained as Minister of Education with a seat in the Cabinet and Hogg (Hailsham) became Secretary of State for Education. All this is relevant to Boyle's writing on education, because he was not only keenly interested in the subject, but he also had many years of experience in a position of power which he later discussed very frankly with Maurice Kogan (Boyle and Crosland, 1971). Kogan puts many excellent questions to Boyle which reveal his position within a Conservative ideology or perhaps outside it:

> Yet his commitment to education, like that of, say, Lord Eccles and Richard Hornby, raises questions for the historians of po-litical ideology. How can we differentiate Boyle from Crosland or, say, Shirley Williams? For on some issues Boyle displays an etatist radicalism which implies more a belief in communal action than in Selsdon man doing it alone, and he sides with many Labour politicians on such issues as the abolition of the death penalty, or race relations. . . . Boyle is heir to no particular Party tradition. His philosophy tells us nothing about the general trend of post-war Conservatism, as Mrs Thatcher's decisions and de-clared policies since his time have made plainer. He is idiosyn-cratically humane and rational and his radicalism is directed at the reduction of inhumanity and irrationalism. It has no other parameters. (Boyle and Crosland, 1971, p. 17)

Boyle was out of step with many Conservatives in his attitude to some aspects of education policy. He refused to condemn all compre-hensive schools, wanting to regard them as a useful experiment. In keeping with his pragmatism he increased the amount in the education budget for research, and encouraged the National Foundation for Edu-cational Research (NFER) study of streaming in primary schools. But though he was on friendly terms with Crosland, the closeness of their views on education has been exaggerated by some writers. Whilst Boyle thought that a bipartisan approach in education was possible, Crosland did not. Boyle regarded selection as inevitable and although he un-doubtedly possessed a strong sense of social justice, and used phrases like 'positive discrimination' which were anathema to many in his Party, he apparently did not see the existence of public schools as a problem in a democratic society. He was much closer to Butler in philosophy than to Crosland. Even his much quoted statement at the beginning of the Newsom Report (1963) is essentially meritocratic. (He said 'all children should have an equal opportunity of acquiring intelligence, and developing their talents and abilities to the full'). He was a highly rational person and wanted to see evidence and have issues fully argued out; he was impressed by what he called 'the dialectic' within the Ministry of Education between those who saw education problems in terms of social justice and those who wanted more technical efficiency. He liked to have long discussions with his officials to explore issues and he clearly learned a good deal from them.

The fact that so many civil servants shared the social and educational background of Conservative Ministers has often been important. Boyle spoke with respect about 'the logic of the service', by which he presumably meant that education tended to follow some aspects (but not all) of social change; if education failed to do so, the service would be both inefficient and unjust. It is interesting to note that Pile, the Permanent Secretary a few years later (1970–76) specified twelve trends or factors which he believed to be the driving force behind educational policy making. They were demographic trends; population movements; children's health; technological change; deprivation; the explosion of knowledge; the impact of the media; the development of educational research; changing ideas about the nature and aims of education; the idea of equality; the demand for participation; and the scarcity of resources (quoted by Lawrence, p. 59). Lawrence in commenting on the order of these trends is critical of DES thinking:

> The extent to which the DES would be deeply concerned with demography and regional variations is not unexpected, though the fact that they are placed at the top of the list does perhaps illustrate the extent to which the DES traditionally saw itself as reactive rather than proactive. (p. 60)

I would suggest, however, that this also illustrates an important difference between Conservative policies and what might be expected from planners: Conservatives react to what is seen to be inevitable (they have what Tony Benn refers to as 'a deep commitment to the benefits of continuity' (Benn, 1989, p. 62). Boyle was reacting to what he saw as the needs of the service at a time of social change; he went further in that direction than any other Tory Minister because he understood the education system better. But he remained a reactor to what he saw as inevitable rather than a visionary planner. This is clear from his own account of the development of the comprehensive idea (Boyle, 1976).

The fact that Boyle eventually left politics is significant. My interpretation would be that at a time when Tory opinion on education was moving to the Right, his own views of such questions as comprehensive schools, teaching methods and curriculum, remained essentially pragmatic and intellectual. He perceived that some kinds of change were essential. Rather than face the bitter conflict which would have been inevitable had he remained as education spokesman, he decided to leave the political field. He remained as Kogan insists a reluctant conservative. In my terms Boyle was a pluralist: he wanted good quality education for all, but he could see the problem of paying for it and, although he was convinced that the 11+ examination was untenable, he remained certain that selection of some kind was desirable.

Boyle is of considerable interest in this study because he illustrates how far a Tory pragmatist can go in the direction of a logic generated by the service itself and still remain a conservative. As Lord Boyle and Vice-Chancellor of the University of Leeds, he chose to sit on the cross benches in the House of Lords. He left a vacancy in the Conservative Party which was, ironically, filled in 1970 by Margaret Thatcher.

Margaret Thatcher

Much of what needs to be said about Margaret Thatcher and education will be reserved for Part II, but here it is interesting to note that when she was Secretary of State for Education, 1970–74, in some respects she behaved in what was the normal way for a Minister in a high-spending department: she demanded and received a large slice of the money available. Yet she was not quite typical. Two anecdotes may be of some significance. The first concerns her visit as Secretary of State to a Schools Council exhibition where she stopped at the display showing the materials of the Humanities Curriculum Project. When she asked what the project's aims were, she was told that it was concerned with teaching about controversial issues. Mrs Thatcher sniffed, said 'In my days we were taught the difference between right and wrong' and passed rapidly on. The second incident was a visit to a new comprehensive community school in Shropshire where she was clearly impressed by the standards and said to the headteacher 'To make this work you will need very special teachers'; the head replied 'Unless we can make the school work with typical teachers, it will be a waste of time.' The first example illustrates the Tory belief that the function of schools is to teach traditional values in an unquestioning way — not to regard them as possible controversial topics for discussion. In the second case, Mrs Thatcher could not think of a very good school as a model for all schools: for her, good schools had to be selective in some significant way, if not of students then of teachers.

Much has been made of the fact that Margaret Thatcher passed a very large number of comprehensive schemes; less mention has been made of the fact that as well as issuing Circular 10/70 (which released LEAs from their obligation to have comprehensive plans) she also did all she could to delay and prevent comprehensive schemes, using Section 13 of the 1944 Act (see Gosden, 1983). There is no evidence that she changed her mind on that aspect of Conservative policy.

Angus Maude

It may be that the most important Conservative influence on education during the years 1951–74 was not a Minister but a veteran of the Tory Party, Angus Maude. From as early as 1953 Maude saw education as a crucial area of policy. In that year he proposed a motion at the Conservative Party Conference deploring the socialist attempt to replace the tripartite system with comprehensive schools. Knight (1990) quotes this incident as evidence to support his view that education controversy started much earlier than the late 1960s, as has often been suggested. Maude criticized Ministers who had allowed 'the system' to dominate policies which had moved ever leftwards since 1944. Knight, in discussing Maude's influence within the Party, uses the term 'Conservative educationalists' which Maude, in an interview with Knight, describes as

> that body of individuals (intellectuals, academic, politicians, educationists, journalists and others) who stood for the preservation of what they saw as the best and most effective of traditional methods and structures, whilst granting the necessity to adapt these to the perceived changing needs of pupils and society. (p. 8)

The key words seem to be *preservation* and *traditional*, but Knight (whose book is a very useful source of Conservative views for this period) goes on to add to the definition:

In the main they have been those individuals who have fought to preserve the grammar school ethos (i.e. strong discipline, high educational standards and streaming by ability). They each believed post-war educational policies to have been increasingly dominated by the socialist principle of compulsory equality — one type of school for all and no selection either within or between schools. This body of individuals was united by a conviction that creativity comes from discipline and individual excellence is best promoted by selection in education. (p. 8–9)

Maude supported the Black Paper writers from 1969 onwards and can be credited with elaborating in various articles the deep-rooted feelings of many less articulate Tories. He transformed many primitive feelings in the deep structure of Conservatism into policies or counter policies at the surface level of political discourse. His chapter in *One Nation* (Alport *et al.*, 1950) is an early example. In it he clearly gives priority to *quality* for a minority rather than spending resources on improving schooling for all.

Schooling can, and must, be provided economically; it can never be provided cheaply . . . An average standard of education which is maintained by lowering the highest standards of quality is worse than inadequate; it cannot even be long maintained. (Quoted in Knight, 1990, p. 12)

In my terms, this is a minimalist argument: Maude was objecting to the move away from the tripartite system (which in practice encouraged lower spending on secondary modern schools) towards comprehensive schools with expensive non-traditional teaching methods which allegedly dragged down the brighter children to the level of the dull ones. He was also insistent that there should continue to be schools outside the state system — partly to provide standards of excellence. The argument was clearly not about the relative efficiency of grammar schools and comprehensive schools, but about the desirability of spending more on the able (selected) children than on 'the average'. This is a very important distinction and an enduring aspect of the Tory Mind: when they lost the argument about selection they were to switch tactics and advocate 'diversity and choice'. The argument about choice was also developing at this stage (notably Sewill, 1959 — see Knight, 1990, p. 14).

Cox and Dyson: The Black Papers

Later, Maude was to give support to Cox and Dyson (editors of the first Black Paper in 1969) and to contribute to the second Black Paper. His message was clear:

> The pendulum has already swung too far. It is necessary now to get very tough with the egalitarians, who would abolish or lower standards out of 'sympathy' with those who fail to measure up to them. We must reject the chimera of equality and proclaim the ideal of quality. The egalitarians whose ideas of social justice are prescriptions for mediocrity and anarchy, must be prevented from having any control over the education of the young. (Cox and Dyson, 1971, p. 40)

In 1972 Cox and Dyson transferred some of their energies to a new institution: the Campaign for the Protection of Educational Standards (CPES). Apart from a general reaction against comprehensive schools and modern methods, Cox and Dyson were particularly concerned about what they saw as a dangerous kind of romanticism — not to be confused with Tory romanticism:

> A bankrupt and dangerous romanticism is at work, with its roots in the early 19th century or even before. 'The road of excess leads to the palace of wisdom' (Blake); 'I am certain of nothing but the holiness of the Heart's affections and the truths of Imagination' (Keats); 'Let Nature be your teacher' (Wordsworth). The essential notion is that men are born free and holy, but are crushed by false pressures from the social world . . . Today, it has become almost a dogma with many educationists, and the unchallenged assumptions behind 'self-expression', 'self-fulfilment' as inalienable goods-in-themselves. (Cox and Dyson, 1969a, p. 78)

Their evidence to the Bullock Committee is also relevant in this context. It is related to the kind of fear of innovation which is often part of the Tory Mind.

According to Knight the translation of right-wing ideas into public debate and later policies was intense during the period of Conservative opposition (1964–70) and reached a peak of publicity with the first two Black Papers. The influence of the Black Papers is shown by Knight (1990) to extend to Margaret Thatcher as Spokesperson for Education in 1969 and as Secretary of State 1970 –74. Knight adds an interesting footnote:

> A number of the propagandists of the educational 'counter-revolution' would be participants in the more global intellectual counter-revolution that also developed in the late 1960s and 70s. For example, Rhodes Boyson and Russell Lewis would meet and collaborate with Ralph Harris, and all three would assemble in the Mount Pelerin Society — a venue in which educational policy has been discussed on many occasions — founded by Hayek to further the post-war revival of classical liberalism. (p. 21)

I have gone into some detail about the beginnings of a swing to the right in the 1960s and early 1970s because it is important not to assume that there was a total change of direction in 1979. The Tory worm had begun to turn much earlier.

Summary

In 1945 Conservatives tended to be carried along with the wave of post-war optimism — anticipating a society which would be an improvement on the 1930s characterized by social upheaval and war with Hitler and Mussolini. By the 1960s this optimism had evaporated and there was a return to more traditional Tory views; the *Black Papers* were a symptom not a cause of this reaction. By 1979, however, traditional Conservatism became mixed up with neo-Liberal thinking in a way which was, as we shall see in chapter 3, not only confusing but also contradictory.

Part II

The Ideological Years 1979–94

Part II of this book covers the fifteen years of Tory rule and its effects on education.

Chapters 3–5 adopt a largely chronological approach; chapter 6 then looks back at the whole period of 1979–94, focusing on Conservative legislation on education, with a critique of the policies for the Thatcher and Major years.

Chapter 3

The Attack on Education 1979–86

The blind, unplanned, uncoordinated wisdom of the market . . . is overwhelmingly superior to the well-researched, rational, systematic, well-meaning, cooperative, science-based, forward-looking, statistically respectable plans of governments . . . The market system is the greatest generator of national wealth known to mankind: coordinating and fulfilling the diverse needs of countless individuals in a way which no human mind or minds could ever comprehend, without coercion, without direction, without bureaucratic interference. (Sir Keith Joseph, 1976, p. 57)

Yet the spirit of the age encourages us to be absolutist. Margaret Thatcher is in tune with this spirit and has perhaps done more than anyone to create it. She likes everything to be clear-cut: absolutely in favour of one thing, absolutely against another. (Francis Pym, 1984, p. 2)

Many analyses of change are incomplete because they regard education in isolation rather than as part of a complex pattern of social, political, economic and cultural developments. In an attempt to avoid that trap, I will begin with a more general description of the phenomenon popularly known as Thatcherism and then move on to a more detailed analysis of the education events — concentrating on those aspects of the policy and legislation which have a particular bearing on 'the Tory Mind' and on changes that took place during that period.

Thatcherism as a Political Phenomenon

One of the models used to explain political change is that significant social changes take place when three factors coincide: a general climate of opinion, specific events and a 'hero' figure prepared to take risks and make the most of the climate of opinion and specific events.

(Kingdon (1984) and Kavanagh (1987) have developed this thesis although they use slightly different terminology.) It seems to me that the onset of Thatcherism from 1975 and more particularly from 1979 could be taken as an illustration of that model in operation: for various reasons which can be briefly reviewed, the climate of political opinion was moving to the right throughout the 1970s; the defeat of the Heath government (twice) in 1974 and of Callaghan in 1979 provided an opportunity for an alternative set of policies; Margaret Thatcher was ready and willing to take the helm and to change direction. Let us examine each of those three factors separately.

1 Climate of opinion

Several political commentators have analyzed the gradual shift, in the 1970s, away from the consensus politics established and generally accepted during and after World War II. The existence for most of the war years of an 'all-party' or national government, which drew up an agenda for a better post-war world, including the Beveridge Report, set the scene for both political parties after the war. The Labour government in 1945 embarked upon a series of ambitious social programmes which the Conservative opposition tended to criticize in detail but not to condemn. When the Labour Party was defeated in 1951, the Churchill administration did not dismantle the welfare state or even begin a programme of denationalization. On the contrary, guarantees were given in Conservative election manifestos about preserving the National Heath Service and continuing with other social reforms. Although it would be wrong to assume that there was no Tory opposition, there was clearly enough support within the Party to justify talking at that stage of consensus which was a continuation of the end of the war optimism as well as continuing the wartime spirit of all parties working together and working with the trade unions. Cooperative, collectivist planning mechanisms which had helped to win the war were retained by both parties, but with less enthusiasm by the Conservatives. Eventually, some controls such as food rationing became contentious and were abandoned, despite the continuing economic problems.

The extent of economic decline in Britain since the war is an area of some dispute among economists, but it is clear that the cost of the war involved sacrificing a large proportion of overseas investments, and by 1945 we could remain solvent only by massive borrowing from the USA on terms which some regarded as humiliating. In addition, much of the industrial plant was obsolete, worn out or destroyed by bombing.

Investment in industry should have been a high priority, but it had to compete with demands for investment for the welfare state (houses, schools, hospitals, and so on) as well as very high costs of defence (at a time when future rivals — Italy, Germany and Japan — were not allowed to use their resources on rearming).

For whatever reasons, Britain's rate of growth was relatively low, our balance of payments was not always healthy and many traditional industries were out-classed by overseas competition. Successive governments from 1945 onwards attempted to find solutions without complete success. The system appeared not to be working. Some right-wing critics, with one eye on the trade unions, began to talk of Britain being 'ungovernable', but some more moderate commentators praised Britain for coping reasonably well, not only with diminished industrial power but with the 'end of Empire'.

Some of the discussions of the 'failure' of British industry were associated with criticisms of Keynesian economics which both parties had generally supported after the war, but which, as early as the 1960s, some Conservatives, including Enoch Powell, were rejecting. The views of Milton Friedman and other monetarists, became more influential, and by 1976 even the Labour Party Prime Minister, James Callaghan, was saying we could not spend our way out of a recession, and his Chancellor of the Exchequer, Denis Healey, introduced measures which looked suspiciously like monetarist solutions.

Related to these economic ideas, the political views of Hayek were, by the 1970s, being advocated by such right-wing groups as the Institute of Economic Affairs (IEA), the Adam Smith Institute and the Centre for Policy Studies (CPS) which had been set up by Margaret Thatcher and Keith Joseph in 1974. Hayek, whose *Road to Serfdom* had been published as early as 1943, but had not been regarded as relevant to the English scene, was, during the 1970s, being used to attack the principles of the welfare state, high taxation, high government spending and the problem of inflation. Hayek and his supporters had consistently advocated free enterprise rather than state controls, limited government action — preferably only defence, and law and order — with everything else being controlled by a free market.

An alternative to the Keynesian consensus economics was lurking in the background, together with a social philosophy which supported criticisms of the welfare system on moral as well as on economic grounds. Individualism seemed to be gaining ground at the expense of collectivism. Denis Healey, in his autobiography, whilst himself rejecting the views of Hayek claims that he was aware of a change in public opinion at that time; James Callaghan, reflecting on 1979, spoke of a 'sea change' (see Marquand in Skidelsky, 1988, p. 165). The public seemed to be ready for new ideas and alternative solutions. The economic picture looked even gloomier after the 1973 rise in the price of oil and the beginnings of a world recession. When the future looks fearsome there is a tendency to look nostalgically to the past and to embrace reactionary solutions; chapter 2 showed that the Tories were not exempt from this.

2 The specific events of 1974 and 1979

In 1970 Edward Heath became Prime Minister. His government was committed to some of the alternative policies mentioned above: lower taxes, risking higher unemployment, non-intervention in industry, together with policies for combatting inflation, including a lower Public Sector Borrowing Requirement (PSBR). He was soon tempted into a series of U-turns, including bailing out Rolls Royce, but his real downfall was caused by his conflict with the National Union of Miners, followed by the three-day week and a General Election fought on the question 'Who governs Britain?' He lost the election and Harold Wilson became Prime Minister in 1974, but handed over to James Callaghan in 1976. Despite his claim of a special relationship with the unions, Callaghan also ran into similar difficulties when he attempted a pay restraint policy which resulted in the 'winter of discontent' 1978–79 with streets left unswept, hospitals functioning badly and, on one much-publicised occasion, the dead being left unburied.

Not only did Callaghan fail to be re-elected, but his inability to manage the economy, and to preserve law and order any better than Heath, provided the event which indicated the failure of consensus policies. The way was open for an alternative set of policy ideas, if a leader — a 'hero' — could be found to introduce them.

3 The 'Hero': Margaret Thatcher

When Heath was defeated in 1974, Margaret Thatcher seemed an unlikely leader of the Conservative Party. Apart from her gender, she was lacking in a number of the crucial criteria for Tory leadership. She was not one of the 'inner circle' of the Party, she had not held any of the major offices of state (her highest achievement had been Secretary of

State for Education 1970–74), and she did not appear to have any real power base nationally or inside the parliamentary party. Her eventual success was due partly to her own determination, but also to what was judged to be a very skilful campaign conducted by the right-wing MP Airey Neave. When Keith Joseph announced that he would not stand against Heath in 1975, Margaret Thatcher became the candidate of the right as well as of those who were simply disenchanted with Heath. On the first ballot she gained 130 votes to Heath's 119; Heath withdrew from the fray, but others entered and on the second ballot the result was Margaret Thatcher 146; Whitelaw 79; Prior 19; Howe 19.

From 1975–79 Margaret Thatcher proved to be a competent leader of the opposition. When Callaghan failed, in 1979, she was in position ready to take over as Prime Minister. Her first Cabinet was a carefully balanced mixture of ex-Heathites and her own right-wing supporters. Policies moved steadily to the right, and gradually more and more of the 'wets' (those still guilty of advocating consensus policies such as Keynesian measures to keep unemployment down) were dismissed or resigned.

At first there was much talk of monetarism as a major aspect of policy, but that panacea gradually gave way to other means of managing the economy, as well as such right-wing policies as privatization (British Telecom, water, etc.). The high rates of interest produced record figures for bankruptcies, and the British share of manufacturing industry fell alarmingly. Margaret Thatcher stuck to her policies uttering such slogans as 'There is no alternative' (TINA) and 'The lady's not for turning.'

By 1981–82 her popularity had sunk to a very low ebb, but it revived during the Falklands Campaign (1982) when she portrayed herself as a great war leader. She won the next General Election in 1983, partly because the Labour opposition was in disarray. She continued with her programme, except that less was now heard of monetarism, and won the 1987 election, having defeated Arthur Scargill, and brought to an end the miners' strike in 1985. She was expected to lose to Labour in 1987 but, despite her personal unpopularity and a good deal of public disapproval of some of her policies, she won — perhaps because the electorate feared an increase in taxes. Those in work were not doing badly; only the minority (3 million or so) unemployed or bankrupt were suffering. Galbraith's thesis of *The Culture of Contentment* (1992) seemed to apply: selfish individualism was triumphing over a concern for the whole community in a very disturbing way. Many had been shocked by Thatcher's statement to the effect that there is no society only individuals, but it seemed that there had been some general acceptance of extreme individualism.

The Impact of Thatcherism on Education 1979–86

In this section I want to analyze the development of Tory thinking on education from 1979 to 1986, partly through what the politicians concerned said and did, and partly through a study of the events themselves, against the background set out at the beginning of this chapter.

Before embarking on the Thatcherite attack on education, it may be helpful to describe the state of the education system in 1979. The 1944 Education Act had changed the nature of secondary education from being a privilege for a few to a right for all. This not only increased the number of pupils involved, but also altered the structure, the ethos of schools, the role of the teacher and, eventually, the curriculum. At first the Labour governments from 1945 onwards gave priority to providing sufficient buildings and teachers. Only later were questions raised about the meaning and purpose of education. Most LEAs had taken the view that the Act had intended different kinds of secondary school — secondary modern and technical as well as the traditional grammar schools — but gradually this view gave way to a general move towards comprehensive schooling (in Conservative as well as Labour Authorities, as Edward Boyle (1970) later showed). Given these massive educational changes in the post-war years it is not surprising that mistakes were made. One of them was to develop very large comprehensive schools which made organization quite different and good order more difficult to achieve. The problems were never as great as right-wing propagandists claimed, but there were serious difficulties, not least in London and other inner city areas, where a major problem was a shortage of teachers and lack of teacher stability.

The second issue was curriculum. The 1944 Act had not specified a national curriculum or even provided any curriculum guidelines (apart from religious education). Curriculum became a school responsibility; some schools coped better than others. Without a national curriculum structure, the way was open for experimentation. One of the lasting Conservative criticisms has been that some teachers have encouraged the idea that 'anything goes', that one taste is as good as any other, that pop culture is as good as traditional culture or that teachers should not impose middle-class standards on their pupils. Accounts of such views have often been exaggerated and were never as widespread as Conservative writers (in the Black Papers and elsewhere) have suggested.

But the William Tyndale School (where teachers allowed children to choose whether to learn to read or not) was not an isolated case.

The 1960s and 1970s were periods of doubt and uncertainty, and for some the uncertainty carried over into teachers' thinking about the purpose of schooling and the curriculum. It is also true that some Training Colleges (later renamed Colleges of Education) and University Departments of Education were for a while over-committed to fashionable theories such as the 'new sociology of education' which called into question traditional practices in schools. A few students may have been influenced by those ideas, but there was never the wholesale capture of the educational establishment that some have suggested, and some fashionable ideas, for example, the Plowden Report's child-centred approach, were strongly resisted by moderate educationists long before the right-wing reacted — for example, *Perspectives on Plowden* (1968) edited by Richard Peters.

However, by 1979, many Conservatives had gained the impression that schools were chaotic and teachers were lax, or — worse still — militant egalitarians who used the classroom for subversive political activities. The right wing feared that schooling had ceased to be a means of promoting order and obedience, and had taken on the role of encouraging the young to be critical of authority and disrespectful. And pupils could not spell.

Other Conservatives were concerned with what they perceived to be poor quality school-leavers. There were now fewer unskilled and semi-skilled jobs available, and recruits for some white-collar positions were being accepted from lower down the range of ability. This meant that school-leavers entering industry became very easy targets for criticism. Some Conservatives said that schools should be encouraged to concentrate more on the basics and spend less time on frills. In addition, schools and teachers were taking the blame for many of the problems of modern industrial society, and the breakdown of the traditional family. After 1968 and the student demonstrations, universities as well as schools were criticized.

These were difficult years for schools and a difficult time for those attempting to run the system. Mistakes were made by both Parties: the Labour Party had made comprehensive schooling compulsory, and therefore politically contentious, at just the time when LEAs were already moving voluntarily in that direction. Their mistake was impatience; the Conservative Party's mistake was being unwilling to face the future. The Great Debate on education, initiated by James Callaghan in 1976, served to confuse rather than clarify educational issues. By 1979 there was much confusion.

Mark Carlisle, Secretary of State for Education (1979–81)

Mark Carlisle was a lawyer who, like many Conservative Education Ministers, had had no previous experience of state education in his political career. He was thought to be one of the 'wet' Heathites in the Cabinet — a one-nation Tory who was regarded as expendable two years later. The 1979 Conservative Manifesto had promised increased parental choice and higher standards. Carlisle's first task was to repeal the 1976 Act which had required LEAs to embark upon plans for comprehensive secondary schools. He was also responsible for issuing the DES document *A Framework for the School Curriculum* (1980a), but that had been well under way before the change of government: it was a bureaucratic, rather than a political statement, also curiously out of step with the more professional HMI publication *A View of the Curriculum* (1980b) which appeared very soon afterwards.

Several years later Mark Carlisle (now Lord Carlisle) stated in a speech to the College of Preceptors that his proudest achievement in education was the Assisted Places Scheme (part of the 1981 Act). He must be a little offended by the fact that several authors (including Kenneth Baker in his autobiography) give the credit for this to Keith Joseph. In fact the APS was a clear attempt to provide a degree of parental choice for some (a small percentage whose children were deemed to be academically able) whilst indicating to parents in general that comprehensive schools were not suitable for academic pupils. I have elsewhere (Lawton, 1992) described Carlisle as a confused moderate, and nothing I have come across since reaching the conclusion has caused me to change my mind. He clearly did not understand the needs of the education service very well, although he did his best to seek adequate funding at a time when cuts in public expenditure were being demanded by monetarists. His stubbornness in that respect contributed to the decision in 1981 to replace him by the economically tougher Keith Joseph.

> Mark Carlisle, who had not been a very effective Education Secretary and leaned to the left, also left the Cabinet — but he did so with courtesy and good humour. (Thatcher, 1993, p. 151)

Education thinking and practice had moved a little to the right under the moderate Carlisle, especially in terms of the consumerist idea of parental choice. We should also remember that throughout his time as Secretary of State, Carlisle had Dr Rhodes Boyson as a Junior Minister at the DES.

Boyson was an obvious right-wing 'minder' for the 'wet' Carlisle. Boyson had once been a Labour Party supporter, but had moved sharply to the right in the 1960s. He became a leading supporter of the Black Papers and a contributor to them. An ex-teacher and headteacher, Boyson had a certain credibility in the field of education, despite a tendency to sloganize rather than to argue, and to be always in search of simplistic solutions. His views carried weight with Tory backbenchers, and he was probably one of the opinion-setters on education in the Tory Party. He had become a consistent advocate of choice in education, including the preservation of grammar schools, and a critic of what he described as low standards of discipline and academic work which he attributed to an emphasis on trendy teaching methods. He was opposed to what he saw as the doctrinaire Labour Party approach towards comprehensive schools and he accused them of being willing to destroy good schools in order to produce comprehensive plans. Some views that he put forward in his own publications, and in the Black Papers, were to become official Party policy later — for example, testing all pupils at age 7, 11 and 14.

Knight (1990) shows that right-wing policies had gained enormous ground during the opposition period 1975–79. Boyson was then also an advocate of promoting choice by means of educational vouchers, a scheme which Keith Joseph was officially to abandon in 1983, but the principle of which (parental choice plus a cash value for each pupil) became official policy in 1988. For Boyson, education was not just a question of efficiency: he blamed modern education for the breakdown of moral standards. He also supported extreme forms of competition such as the publication of school examination and test results in League Tables, which also became a feature of the 1988 Act.

During these years (1979–81) 'excellence' (for some) began to be seen as an alternative to better provision for all. Another Conservative who was significant in this 'excellence' campaign was Stuart Sexton, the official education policy adviser to the Conservative Party in opposition 1975–79, and then adviser to both Mark Carlisle and Keith Joseph when they became Education Secretary. Apart from being a campaigner for vouchers and parental choice, Sexton was particularly involved in drafting and promoting the Assisted Place Scheme. (See Knight, 1990, for details.) Sexton clearly believed that *all* schools should be independent: in my terms he was a perfect example of a privatizer.

According to Wapshott and Brock (1983) there was little Cabinet discussion of education in the Carlisle years (1979–81); but it is clear that there was a good deal of right-wing 'theorizing' going on behind the scenes. Education opinion within the Conservative Party was moving steadily to the right. After the 1980 Act, Carlisle was increasingly criticized by the right: for example, Alan Howarth at the Conservative Research Department felt that the Act did not go far enough, especially on the issue of vouchers. According to Knight (1990, p. 143) Howarth was listening to the right-wing ideas of Alfred Sherman, a believer in the free market and the minimal state. Another who pressed for Carlisle's replacement by someone more right wing was Teresa Gorman, an ex-teacher, but more significantly a member of the Adam Smith Club, FEVER (Friends of the Education Voucher Experiment in Representative Regions) and the CPS: she represented the ideas of the free marketeers who regarded Carlisle as one of the old guard of Tory paternalists. The Selsdon Group, which was campaigning for vouchers, included Nicholas Ridley and was associated with the Freedom Group — a pressure group for privatization outside education.

Sir Keith Joseph, Secretary of State for Education (1981–86)

Margaret Thatcher said that Keith Joseph had asked to move to education:

> Keith Joseph had told me that he wished to move from Industry. With his belief that there was an anti-enterprise culture which had harmed Britain's economic performance over the years, it was natural that Keith should now wish to go to Education where that culture had taken deep roots. (Thatcher (1993), p. 151)

According to Harry Judge (1984), during the Joseph era 'the mood and pace of education policy were changed'; a view from another perspective (Knight, 1990) agrees completely. Joseph wanted to change the whole nature of the education service, emphasizing choice and excellence rather than what he saw as drab uniformity and mediocrity in comprehensive schools. A part of the new vision (strongly influenced by David Young) was that technical and vocational dimensions of secondary education should be strengthened. Joseph was also particularly concerned that the system had appeared to offer so little to the 'bottom 40 per cent' of the ability range: they had an unsuitable curriculum, no school-leaving certificate, and very poor preparation for work and adult life. Joseph wanted 'good schools for all' (the title of his 1981 address to Conservative Party Conference), but this did not mean the same for all. Good basic education and training for the less able could be better and cheaper, according to Joseph, if it were separated from academic secondary education. Sexton advised him that these views were quite compatible with market solutions for education. Selection would be an important element for reasons of cost and excellence: 'relevance' and 'fitness for purpose' became key concepts.

Throughout his time at the DES, however, Joseph, who was at heart a privatizer, was tortured by doubts about running a statist system:

> We have a bloody State system, I wish we hadn't got. I wish we'd taken a different route in 1870. We got the ruddy state involved. I don't want it. I don't think we know how to do it. I certainly don't think Secretaries of State know anything about it. But we are landed with it. If we could go back to 1870, I would take a different route. We've got compulsory education, which is a responsibility of hideous importance, and we tyrannise children to do that which they don't want, and we don't produce results. (Interview with Stephen Ball, 1990, p. 62)

Knight, who interviewed Joseph, suggests that he was concerned that there was a kind of conspiracy operating within the education service:

> Here Joseph shared a view common to all Conservative Educationists: that education had seen an unholy alliance of socialists, bureaucrats, planners and Directors of Education acting against the true interests and wishes of the nation's children and parents by their imposition on the schools of an ideology [equality of condition] based on utopian dreams of universal cooperation and brotherhood. (Knight, 1990, p. 155)

It was time for the education consensus to be abandoned: a new policy was hammered out, with the assistance of the Centre for Policy Studies Education Study Group (CPSESG). The Group stated:

> We need to make our education system proof against the irreversible structural changes now intended by the Labour Party which is now committed to the abolition of independent schools . . . with compulsory enforcement of mixed ability teaching and the destruction of religious and single sex schools. (Knight, 1990, p. 154)

The CPS document went on to recommend: a range of examinations to cater for diverse needs of children; more grouping by ability; more parental choice; flexible transfer arrangements encouraging pupils to change schools; more information about schools — including examination results; more variety of types of schools should be encouraged. They were also very anxious that vouchers should be made available to enable parents to choose either state or independent schools, and that schools with good sixth forms should be retained.

Many of these ideas coincided with Keith Joseph's intuitive judgments. Yet the first recommendation was soon countered by Joseph's decision to proceed with a single school-leaving examination — the GCSE. The Right did, however, continue to campaign against the new examination, putting pressure on Baker to cancel the GCSE plans and later calling for a return to 'O'-Level standards. They regarded a single examination as a betrayal of the sacred policy of differentiation. Knight has argued that on most issues, however, the CPS views, many of them straight out of the Black Papers, became official policy.

In 1982, Joseph's slogan at the North of England Conference was 'more effective education for all children'. 'Effective' for Joseph meant different according to ability, with more 'practical' education for the less able. To many this seemed to be a new version of 'basics', plus a campaign to eliminate mixed-ability teaching. A new key word was *differentiated*. Knight (1990) refers to Joseph's policies of 'the new selection' together with a more utilitarian approach to education (p. 155) — in my terms 'minimalism'. But the DES successfully steered Joseph away from vouchers, for practical reasons, although intellectually Joseph was still a convinced privatizer. Margaret Thatcher supported him completely:

> In education, Keith Joseph had begun what would be a long process of reform. Falling school rolls had allowed us to increase to record levels public spending per pupil and to achieve the best ever pupil–teacher ratios. But extra resources only permit improved standards: they do not ensure them. So Keith was pressing for changes in teacher training. He was issuing new guidelines for the school curriculum. Keith and I were also anxious to do something more to increase parents' power to choose by seriously investigating the possibilities of vouchers or at least a combination of 'open enrolment' and 'per capita funding', that is a kind of voucher applying just to the state sector. (Thatcher, 1993, pp. 279–80).

In preparation for the 1983 Election, Geoffrey Howe (Chancellor of the Exchequer) set up yet another education group — the Conservative Education Policy Group (CEPG) chaired by Lord Beloff, who later told Knight:

> I adhered to the philosophy *more means worse*. There had been a considerable ebb to and fro as to what constituted a teacher in schools. The development of education as a profession had concentrated on things like psychology and sociology, which helped the teacher as a communicator but did little to help teachers as educators. I believed teachers should be *skilled scholars*. I had long felt that educational standards had been falling, particularly in modern language teaching and in standards of teacher training. (1990, p. 161)

The recommendations of the CEPG included better moral and religious education as well as 'a more vocational slant to the curriculum', retaining GCE and better teacher training. But not vouchers. The 1983 manifesto described Conservative education policy as 'the pursuit of excellence'. For some time Beloff remained an important influence within the Conservative Party. He believed in a national curriculum and in the kind of curriculum which would prepare young people for citizenship. But he was eventually to become a critic of later Conservative policies on education.

After the Conservative victory in 1983, Keith Joseph remained as Secretary of State but Boyson was replaced by Bob Dunne, one of his disciples and also a close associate of Stuart Sexton. (He distinguished himself later by not being able to remember for his *Who's Who* entry at which university he had studied for a degree.) This was a period characterized by some as 'the new vocationalism', with not only different curricula for different kinds of pupil, but different curricula which would anticipate their occupational destinations. Selection had to be part of this plan. And schooling should be more clearly related to the needs of industry — although there was not complete agreement about what they were.

Another of Joseph's concerns was the quality of teachers (and of teacher training). His White Paper *Teaching Quality* (DES, 1983) is a positive indication of that concern; on the negative side, Joseph was always unpopular with the teaching profession because they interpreted his concern — especially his theme of ineffective teachers — as carping criticism.

Joseph's 1984 North of England speech signalled three changes in educational policy: firstly, higher standards for all (with special efforts to lift the bottom 40 per cent); secondly, in examinations, a shift from norm referencing to criterion referencing (absolute standards), especially for the GCSE (partly to give industrialists more specific information about the achievements of future employees); and, finally, clearly-defined curriculum objectives agreed by all (including parents and employers), thus encouraging greater 'relevance'. At this time, Joseph was being influenced by the views of Lord Young who had not only introduced TVEI (the Technical and Vocational Education Initiative) with Department of Industry money, but was also concerned to make schooling generally more relevant to the needs of industry and commerce.

The emphasis on relevance and vocationalism did not please everyone in the Party, including Roger Scruton, who resisted the idea of education as a market commodity (Knight, 1990, p. 170). This indicates an important difference between two Conservative viewpoints — that of the old humanists and the industrial trainers. At this time Joseph was on the side of relevance.

Much of Joseph's educational thinking at this stage was contained in a DES publication *Better Schools* (1985) which Knight describes as a 'kind of modern Black Paper'. It was an up-dated version of Joseph's 1984 North of England speech and contained a restatement of aims previously listed in *The School Curriculum* (DES, 1981, p. 1):

1   To help pupils to develop lively, enquiring minds, the ability to question and argue rationally and to apply themselves to tasks and physical skills.
2   To help pupils to acquire understanding, knowledge and skills relevant to adult life and employment in a fast-changing world.
3   To help pupils to use language and number effectively.
4   To help pupils to develop personal moral values, respect for religious values, and tolerance of other races, religions and ways of life.
5   To help pupils to understand the world in which they live, and the inter-dependence of individuals, groups and nations.
6   To help pupils to appreciate human achievements and aspirations.

Soon after the publication of *Better Schools*, Joseph announced his wish to retire at the next election.

In those years, 1979–86, there had been a steady drift not only to the right but to vocationalism. There was no coherent policy, partly because there was still conflict among the Conservatives themselves. In addition, Keith Joseph, who was committed ideologically to anti-statist, privatizing policies, found himself in charge of the state system. He was on several occasions convinced by his officials (Walter Ulrich often gets the credit) that some right-wing policies were impracticable — the vouchers issue was perhaps his most important 'failure' in this respect.

Beloff, Scruton and others, were not convinced that simply exposing education to market forces would produce the kind of education service needed. By now, however, such voices were in a minority within the Party: as we shall see in chapters 4 and 5, even those who thought of themselves as moderate and traditionalist began to use the language of 'choice and the market'. Selection had also made a strong comeback as a Tory principle, sometimes under the new cloak of *differentiation*. When Joseph retired from Education to go to the House of Lords, he was able to revert to a purer Privatizer position and occasionally found it necessary to criticize his successor's policies — especially the National Curriculum.

Chapter 4

The Baker Years 1986–89

> I was . . . particularly sad to see Keith go in May 1986 and be replaced by Kenneth Baker. Kenneth is a most civilised man with an agreeably sunny disposition, but not even his greatest friends would describe him as either a profound political thinker or a man with a mastery of detail. His instinctive answer to any problem is to throw glossy P.R. and large quantities of money at it, and his favoured brand of politics is the instant response to the cry of the moment. It would have been hard to imagine anyone less like Keith. More to the point, it was hard to imagine that we would get from Kenneth the fundamental thinking about education reform that I was sure was needed. (Nigel Lawson, 1992, p. 606)

This period will be remembered above all for the 1988 Education Reform Act (ERA). In some respects ERA was the creation of Kenneth Baker who took over as Secretary of State when Keith Joseph stepped down in 1986. Baker is an interesting example of a Conservative who changed during the Thatcher years. In 1979 he was not only considered to be a Heathite, but a particularly 'wet' one. He had been Heath's Parliamentary Private Secretary (1974–75) and had voted for him in the 1975 leadership contest. Probably for that reason he was given no shadow responsibility during the opposition years (1975–79) and he was not offered even a junior post in the first Thatcher administration in 1979. Yet by 1988 he appeared to be a fully-fledged Thatcherite, devoted to the idea of parental choice and bent upon opening up education to market forces. It will be interesting to analyze what took place that might account for this shift which was, in my view, a genuine change of mind rather than political expedience.

Until his autobiography appeared in September 1993, I had assumed that Kenneth Baker was a pluralist in education, more interested in improving the central machinery of the DES (as it then was) than in extending market ideas into education. The evidence of his book makes it essential to rethink that view. I also find it necessary to question the opinion that Baker was simply an ambitious politician using education as a stepping stone to more prestigious Cabinet posts. There is reason to believe that he was genuinely interested in education. Baker mentions in his autobiography that in 1975 he became Chairman of the Hansard Society. This is not a high-profile position; it is one which is usually occupied by someone with a real concern that young people should be better informed about the workings of Parliament. I first met Kenneth Baker in 1980 during his period as Chairman of the Hansard Society: the Institute of Education had been given a grant involving the Hansard Society for a project concerned with the promotion of some aspects of political literacy; after the grant had been made, Kenneth Baker invited the two researchers and me (as the one responsible for the budget) to the House of Commons to have lunch with him and to tell him about the aims of the project. He showed himself to be very concerned about the low level of knowledge about politics and Parliament among young people (as well as being generally well informed about education). He was also mildly critical — in an open but not snide way — of the fact that Margaret Thatcher was giving Mark Carlisle, then the Secretary of State for Education, a hard time. He had absolutely nothing to gain from this exchange of views, except that he was clearly anxious to learn. My colleagues and I took this to be evidence of a commitment to education which was lacking in many of his colleagues. There is more evidence from his autobiography which I will refer to later in this chapter.

Meanwhile, it would be relevant to review briefly Baker's career before he became Education Secretary. Baker's father had been a civil servant, but on leaving university, Kenneth Baker sought a job in industry. His own account of those years would seem to indicate that he was more impressed by the world of business and commerce than what he knew of Whitehall. His first government position as a junior minister in the Civil Service Department (1972–74) may have confirmed his prejudices. He developed a keen interest in making better use of information technology in bureaucratic organizations and in schools. He felt that there was a need for Britain to develop in this field if we were to keep up with, or even to get ahead of, our overseas competitors. He became an advocate for improving the use of technology in industry, government and education. And, in his own words, he wrote his own ministerial job specification as Minister of State for Industry and Information Technology.

He began to admire Margaret Thatcher, even when she was at her most awful during the Falklands campaign. And he displayed strong Thatcherite tendencies when he was put in charge of British Telecom privatization in 1981. He took on this task with enthusiasm and writes about the policy of privatizing a great national monopoly as though he had no doubts about it at all. In April 1981 he embarked on the programme to have a computer in every school — more evidence of his interest in education. But he also observed that the DES was very lukewarm on his 'micros in schools' project: he thought they were reluctant to take any initiative in technology education. A further perception was that the DES had no real control over what went on in schools.

In the 1984 reshuffle, Baker moved sideways to become Minister of State for Local Government, which gave him another opportunity to get involved in local education politics: as part of the reorganization of local government, the GLC was abolished, leaving the Inner London Education Authority vulnerable to later attacks. He seemed to share Thatcher's dislike of large, high-spending local authorities. He was rewarded in 1985 by being promoted to Secretary of State for the Environment. Once again he showed himself to be keen on privatization — this time of water. An ominous characteristic for a future Education Secretary.

By 1986 Keith Joseph had indicated to the Prime Minister that he had spent long enough at the DES. Kenneth Baker tells us (and there is no reason to disbelieve him) that he was keen to transfer from Environment to Education. It was a post he really wanted; a subject which interested him very much. His wish was granted.

Four chapters of Baker's *The Turbulent Years* (1993) are devoted to his years at the DES. He saw the Department as an immense challenge:

> No-one had yet grasped the nettle of a major legislative overhaul. While Keith Joseph had planted many of the seeds for what would become elements of the Education Reform Bill, I realised that the scale of the problem could only be tackled by a coherent national programme, and time was not on our side. I knew what I wanted in the package, and I knew I would have to drive it through my Department, persuade the Prime Minister and colleagues that it should be adopted in the form I wanted, and then steer a major piece of legislation through Parliament and around all the obstacles which the vested education interests would throw in its way. (p. 164)

He was already seeing 'vested interests' in education as the enemy — a typical feature of the Tory Mind. His diagnosis of the situation was that education had lost its way in the 1960s, abandoning the selective system of grammar, technical and secondary modern schools for the untried comprehensive system.

We began to make comparisons with other countries particularly Germany and France. In West Germany, nine out of ten sixteen year olds got a Hauptschule certificate covering maths, German, a foreign language and two other subjects. The equivalent in England was the CSE Grade 4, and only four out of ten English school leavers achieved this standard. (p. 165)

Baker neglects to tell us who the 'we' were — this could have been officials at the DES or, more likely, some of his more politically oriented advisers such as Sig Prais at the National Institute for Economic Studies. The diagnosis was reasonable to some extent, but instead of pursuing the comparison with further analysis, he immediately resorted to slogans: his solution would be based on 'standards and choice'. By now Baker had adopted the right-wing language of the Black Papers (1969 and 1970) (see chapter 2).

In Baker's view standards were to be achieved by the national curriculum and testing at 7, 11 and 14 (as had been recommended by Rhodes Boyson and the Black Paper writers nearly twenty years before ERA). Choice would be achieved by City Technology Colleges and Grant Maintained Schools, together with Local Management of Schools (LMS) and open enrolment. But he anticipated possible criticisms by declaring that education must be for all levels of ability:

The real test of an education system is how it deals with the children of average and below-average ability and how it can open for them the doors of opportunity. (p. 165)

Baker has some interesting remarks to make about the ministerial colleagues he inherited from Joseph: namely, Chris Patten, George Walden and Bob Dunn:

Relations between Chris and Bob were poor because they came from opposite wings of the Party, an antipathy reinforced by what Bob saw as Chris's inclination to side with leftish civil servants, and what Chris saw as Bob's reliance on Stuart Sexton, Keith Joseph's right-wing Political Adviser. (p. 166)

In my terms this was a clash between a pluralist (Chris Patten) and the privatizers (Sexton and Dunn). It is also interesting to note that Baker talks of 'leftish civil servants'. Another characteristic of the Tory Mind is to see any civil servant who puts a different point of view as left wing. Baker blames them for persuading Joseph that vouchers were not possible: the Wykhamist Walter Ulrich is singled out as an example of bureaucracy obstructing the political will. But Baker tells us that he soon put him in his place. (It came as a surprise to many observers of the DES that Ulrich was seen as left wing — unless left wing means anyone disagreeing with extreme right policies.) It may be that Baker was trying to distance himself from both left and right within the Party in order to present himself as the perfectly balanced modern One-Nation Conservative. I have suggested elsewhere (1992) that this is precisely what Baker had to do in order to make the National Curriculum acceptable to three groups within the Party — the privatizers, the minimalists and the pluralists — and he had to make concessions to each group.

Baker also inherited from Keith Joseph the idea that the DES was part of a left-wing consortium or conspiracy:

> Ministerial morale was also low, due in no small part to an inability to push distinctly Conservative policies past powerful civil servants' opposition. Of all Whitehall Departments, the DES was among those with the strongest in-house ideology. There was a clear 1960s ethos and a very clear agenda which permeated virtually all the civil servants. It was rooted in 'progressive' orthodoxies, in egalitarianism and in the comprehensive school system. It was devoutly anti-excellence, anti-selection, and anti-market. The DES represented perfectly the theory of 'producer capture', whereby the interests of the producer prevail over the interests of the consumer. Not only was the Department in league with the teacher unions, University Departments of Education, teacher training theories [sic], and local authorities, it also acted as their protector against any threats which Ministers might pose. If the civil servants were the guardians of this culture, then Her Majesty's Inspectors of Education [sic] were its priesthood. (p. 168)

One of Baker's first tasks was to resolve the teachers' pay dispute which Joseph had failed to settle. Baker abandoned the Burnham machinery, replacing it first by an Interim Advisory Committee and then the Review Body by means of the Teachers' Pay and Conditions Act (1987). He then began thinking about further legislation which was required. Education was one of the priorities for the 1987 General Election and Mrs Thatcher agreed after the election that promises should be converted into action:

I made no change at Education where Ken Baker would make up in presentational flair whatever he lacked in attention to detail, nor Environment where Nick Ridley was obviously the right man to implement the housing reforms ... These two areas — schools and housing — were those in which we were proposing the most far-reaching changes. (Thatcher, 1993, p. 589)

In her autobiography, Lady Thatcher spends some time expounding her educational priorities — which are splendid indicators of Tory prejudices:

I had always been an advocate of relatively small schools as against the giant, characterless comprehensives. I also believed that too many teachers were less competent and more ideological than their predecessors. I distrusted the new 'child-centred' teaching techniques, the emphasis on imaginative engagement rather than learning facts, and the modern tendency to blur the lines of discrete subjects and incorporate them in wider, less definable entities like 'humanities'. And I knew from parents, employers and pupils themselves that too many people left school without a basic knowledge of reading, writing and arithmetic. But it would be no easy matter to change for the better what happened in schools. (p. 590)

As we shall see, Baker appeared to agree with many of these views. He was certainly required to operate in an awareness of them.

Whilst the 1988 Act was dominated by the right-wing, anti-planning, notion of parental choice, there is also a centralizing aspect of the ERA in the form of the National Curriculum. This was only acceptable to privatizers if they saw the National Curriculum as a method of producing assessment data, school by school, which could be published and which allowed parents to make reasoned choices between schools. The National Curriculum would thus become a market mechanism. Those who saw the National Curriculum in this way, including Margaret Thatcher, wanted simple tests, probably confined to the three core subjects. But Baker was also anxious to carry through his declared intention of having a broad entitlement curriculum (probably derived from his discussions with the Senior Chief Inspector, Eric Bolton). Baker opposed Thatcher on this issue, as well as on the form that National Curriculum assessment should take. And he won the battle — but not the war.

In his book, Kenneth Baker hardly mentions the Cabinet Committee on Education, chaired by the Prime Minister. Nigel Lawson's account of the interplay of ideas in this Committee is of some Lawson interest. First he interfered by commissioning one of his own Treasury civil servants, John Anson, to write a Paper on education reform; then the Chancellor of the Exchequer pushed his own point of view (on education not on expenditure) against those of Baker:

> The Cabinet Sub-Committee on Education Reform proceeded in a way unlike any other on which I have served. The process would start by Margaret putting forward various ideas — in addition to the Anson Paper she had the No. 10 Policy Group heavily involved in the subject, and its then head, Brian Griffiths, was engaged in little else at this time — and there would be a general discussion, to which I would contribute my four-pennyworth. At the end of it, Margaret would sum up and give Kenneth his marching orders. He would then return to the next meeting with a worked out proposal which bore little resemblance to what everyone else recalled as having been agreed at the previous meeting, and owed rather more to his officials at the DES. After receiving a metaphorical handbagging for his pains, he would then come back with something that corresponded more closely to her ideas . . . (Lawson, 1992, pp. 609–10)

Nigel Lawson wanted to be much tougher on the LEAs and cut them out of the funding arrangements altogether. But Margaret Thatcher was more cautious.

On the National Curriculum Margaret Thatcher's own account (1993) is very informative and gives many detailed insights into Conservative views of knowledge and schooling:

> . . . the national curriculum — the most important centralising measure — soon ran into difficulties. I never envisaged that we would end up with the bureaucracy and the thicket of prescriptive measures which eventually emerged. I wanted the DES to concentrate on establishing a basic syllabus for English, mathematics and science with simple tests to show what pupils knew. (p. 593)

Mrs Thatcher felt that Baker had let the National Curriculum get into the wrong hands: 'the original simplicity of the scheme had been lost and the influence of HMI and the teachers' unions was manifest' (p. 594). She was particularly critical of the TGAT Report:

> The next problem arose from the Report by the Task Group on Assessment and Testing which we had established in July 1987 to advise on the practical considerations which would govern assessment, including testing, within the national curriculum. Ken Baker warmly welcomed the Report. Whether he had read it properly I do not know: if he had it says much for his stamina. Certainly I had no opportunity to do so before agreeing to its publication, ·having simply been presented with this weighty, jargon-filled document in my overnight box with a deadline for publication the following day. The fact that it was then welcomed by the Labour Party, the National Union of Teachers and the *Times Educational Supplement* was enough to confirm for me that its approach was suspect. It proposed an elaborate and complex system of assessment — teacher-dominated and uncosted. It adopted the 'diagnostic' view of tests, placed the emphasis on teachers doing their own assessment and was written in an impenetrable educationalist jargon. I minuted my concerns to Ken Baker but by now, of course, it had been published and was already the subject of consultation. (pp. 594–95)

She did not like the mathematics curriculum when it appeared: 'a small mountain . . . a complicated array of "levels", "attainment targets" and . . . "tasks"' (p. 595). She was also very disappointed with the English curriculum: 'although there was acceptance of a place for Standard English, the traditional learning of grammar and learning by heart, which I considered vital for memory training, seemed to find no favour' (p. 395). But most of all, she disliked the proposals from the History Working Party:

> Though not an historian myself, I had a very clear — and I had naively imagined uncontroversial — idea of what history was. History is an account of what happened in the past. Learning history, therefore, requires knowledge of events. It is impossible to make sense of such events without absorbing sufficient factual information and without being able to place matters in a clear chronological framework — which means knowing dates. No amount of imaginative sympathy for historical characters or situations can be a substitute for the initially tedious but ultimately rewarding business of memorizing . . . (p. 595)

Baker's account of this story refers to some disputes with the Prime Minister but gives the impression that he generally got his own way on the National Curriculum and assessment. But his own way was already tempered by the need to keep the rest of the Cabinet reasonably happy, as well as to avoid a revolt by Parliamentary right wingers. Although Baker had moved a long way in the direction of the privatizers, he still retained some of the pluralist ideals such as a broad entitlement curriculum *for all*. He failed to spot the incompatibility of the two positions: the parental choice of the privatizers (which inevitably means differences in quality) and the ideal of quality education for all. If parental choice is meaningful, parents must be allowed to choose between better and worse schools; if they are merely being allowed to choose between different kinds of 'good' (music and art, for example) then why publish league tables of achievement designed to demonstrate differences in quality? Eventually every Conservative politician has to choose between the 'ladder of opportunity' (selecting *some* for superior education) and 'the broad highway' (devising a quality system for all). Baker was not alone in trying to have it both ways — the great Tory double-think on education is that you can have selection *and* quality for all. Baker was lucky to be able to escape from the DES before that inconsistency became all too clear. As we shall see, his successors as Secretary of State for Education, have tended to go for a selective system, although often trying to disguise the fact.

Another of the ideological contradictions in the 1988 Act concerned higher education. Traditionally Tories have expressed a preference for 'independent institutions' (see chapter 1); but the effect of the ERA was to reduce the autonomy of universities and to make them ever more directly accountable to the Secretary of State. The University Grants Committee (UGC) which consisted largely of university professors was replaced by the Universities Funding Council (UFC) with a much larger number of members appointed by the Secretary of State from industry and commerce. The intention was to control expenditure and policy rather than to share out funds between universities and allow them to decide policy. Universities could no longer expect to receive public funds without much tighter controls over how it was spent — it became much more like a contractual relationship with the paymaster calling the tune. These changes were condemned by many outside observers: for example, Stuart Maclure (1989) complained that long-standing conventions had been swept away, including the idea of universities as independent centres of learning and research 'capable of standing out against government and society and offering critical judgments of varying objectivity, informed by learning . . . instead, universities are made the servants of the state' (p. 93). Maurice Kogan (1989) criticized the new arrangements as 'managerialism'. This policy was a departure from traditional Tory views, but rapidly became an accepted doctrine of the new Tory Mind.

Another part of the ERA was concerned with the Inner London Education Authority (ILEA). The effect of the Act was to abolish the ILEA which Baker had long regarded as the worst possible example of a high-spending, left-wing Authority. Other Conservatives, however, saw the abolition of the ILEA as part of a desirable policy of attacking all LEAs and reducing their powers. The Hillgate Group (1987), just before the Act, proposed that schools should be released from the control of local government and financed by direct grant from central funds. This is, of course, exactly what happened as a result of other sections of the Act — especially those concerning Grant Maintained Schools and City Technology Colleges. Sheila Lawlor (1988) was equally frank about CPS views in *Away With LEAs: ILEA abolition as a pilot.*

The ERA (1988) should be seen both as the work of Kenneth Baker and also as an expression of the Tory Mind. Kenneth Baker put through an Act which Joseph would not have, but Baker was working within a general climate of opinion as well as reacting to the specific conditions operating at that time. The dominant value expressed in the Act was the consumerist parental choice which inevitably produces differences in quality and covert selection. Whereas the 1944 Act had to some extent moved away from social selection to academic selection (from social class dominance to meritocratic values), the 1988 Act partly reversed that process. Selection would take place, but the main criterion would not be academic achievement (the old 11+ test) but the more subtle social process of giving tremendous advantages to those who could play the system effectively — the more knowledgable and more affluent middle classes. To those that have, more shall be given. Moreover, the Scottish experience of the effects of choice since 1981 provides ample evidence to show that parental choice is a very poor alternative to a planned system (Adler, 1993; Adler *et al.*, 1989; Willms and Echols, 1992).

Baker is also interesting because he moved from being a convinced supporter of Heath in the 1970s to being converted to Thatcherism in the 1980s. He began using the language of the market in education, and increasingly saw the solution to educational problems in terms of parental choice and competition between schools. Yet he still hankered after a One Nation policy — he kept on saying he wanted quality for all children, apparently unable to see that his policies were essentially divisive. Halsey, in an interesting essay on Thatcherism, picked out Baker's ERA as an example of that divisiveness:

> The educational problem as a transmission of agreed social values integrating new national, ethnic and international communities is vastly more urgent and complex than it was when Durkheim laid out the crucial role for schools and school teachers in the French Third Republic. Kenneth Baker's reforms seem more likely to divide than to unite Britain at the end of the 20th century. (in Skidelsky, 1988, p. 185)

From 1986–89 traditional Tory values in education were significantly challenged by neo-liberalism and Baker's 'conversion' is interesting as a possible example of what David Marquand had in mind in his chapter 'The Paradoxes of Thatcherism':

> The other day I had the privilege of talking to a rather senior high Tory who said he thought the battle between wets and drys in the Cabinet was now over. There were no wets; the wets had been smashed to pieces. Everybody accepted the dry economic diagnosis; and everyone agreed with the dry economic cure. But, he went on, there is a very acute tension within the government even so. The real line of cleavage . . . is between those who want to sell off every cathedral close to Tescos in the name of the free market, and those who want to preserve them in the name of being British, or at least of being English: between those who believe in economic liberalism without qualification, and those who wish to erect barriers to market forces, not in the name of wet compassion but in the name of continuity, community and nation. (in Skidelsky, 1988, p. 172)

But Baker was never 100 per cent dry: not only did he steer through a centralist national curriculum, but he fought the Prime Minister to retain a broad, balanced national curriculum — a pluralist measure — rather than accept the minimalist core curriculum. He also defended the GCSE against fierce right-wing attacks mounted by Brian Griffiths and others in the CPS. Other contradictions included the fact that he strongly supported higher education but attacked tenure and university autonomy. A course of action which some would regard as the complete reverse of the kind of Toryism which believes in diffusion of power. Baker not only represents the changing face of Conservatism in the 1980s, he is an exemplar of Tory confusion on education.

In this chapter I have relied heavily on Baker's own speeches and his autobiography. This is clearly a dangerous practice, but I have also compared Baker's own version of events with those of the more right-wing Nigel Lawson as well as with Margaret Thatcher's memoirs. The comparisons are interesting and reveal subtle variations in the Tory Mind during the late 1980s.

Annex to Chapter 4

Kenneth Baker was more open about his likes and dislikes in education than most politicians. I have attempted a content analysis of his speeches and publications (his autobiography is particularly revealing), and I put forward the following two lists which are, I suggest, indications of the Tory Mind — or at least the Baker version of it — that is, one who was in 1979 a pluralist, retained many of those characteristics but increasingly used the language and ideas of the privatizers (choice and the market). (The page references refer to Baker (1993).)

Table 1: Kenneth Baker's likes and dislikes in education

Likes	Dislikes
Assisted Places Scheme (p. 163) (p. 180)	Local Education Authorities (p. 163)
Coherent national programme (p. 164)	Comprehensive schools (p. 165)
Tripartite system (p. 164)	
'Standards and Choice' (p. 165)	The 1960s ethos: progressive orthodoxies — egalitarianism (p. 168)
Testing (p. 178)	
Excellence, selection, the market (p. 180)	Producer capture (p. 168)
	HMI (p. 168)
Good sex education (p. 170)	Striking teachers (p. 172)
Contracts (p. 173)	Teacher Unions (p. 175)
The Professional Association of Teachers (p. 175)	The Educational Establishment (p. 182)
Technology in the curriculum (p. 177)	Core curriculum (p. 193)
Magnet Schools (p. 178)	Everyday use of language (p. 200)
Output Measures (p. 181)	Casual and relaxed English (p. 201)
Broad and balanced curriculum (p. 189)	Colloquial inaccuracies (p. 201)
	Creative writing (p. 200)
A canon in English (p. 190)	
Grammar (p. 190)	Less rigorous environmental studies (p. 193)
Standard English (p. 201)	
	GMS Fees (p. 195)
Punctuation and spelling (p. 200)	
	Prizes for everyone (p. 199)
Memorizing poetry and spelling (p. 201)	Calculators, problem-solving and child-centred approaches (p. 203)
Foreign language (p. 193)	
History (events) (p. 193)	Historical imagination (empathy) (p. 206)
Geography (facts) (p. 193)	Social separation of a divided educational market (p. 210)
Grant Maintained Schools (p. 195)	ILEA (p. 223)

Attainment Targets (p. 196)

Publication of test results
(p. 199)
Maths — long division and
tables (p. 203)

Historical facts and chronology
(p. 206)
Parental choice (p. 210)

Decentralization (from hub to
rim) (p. 210)
LMS (p. 210)
Governors (p. 210)
Per capita funding (p. 213)
Open enrolment (p. 213)

Longer school day (p. 353)

Expansion of HE (p. 235)

HE independent of LEAs
(p. 235)

Student loans (p. 236)

Expansion of FE (p. 245)

Licensed teachers and articled
teachers (p. 247)

Militant students (p. 232)

The HE Unit of Resource
(p. 234)

The autonomy of universities
(p. 234)
Academic tenure (p. 242)

Chapter 5

From Confusion to Chaos 1989–94

The national curriculum is in danger of being changed from a means for improvement to an instrument for regression. A striking feature of this development is that the quality of the debate and thinking . . . is alarmingly low. One characteristic of the weak thinking is the 'bogeymen' approach. A group or trend is identified — the 'educational establishment' or 'woolly left-wing thinking' — and then any idea, any criticism, and difficulty is dismissed by being ascribed to this bogey, so that it is not necessary to think seriously about it . . . A second characteristic is the neglect of evidence . . . a third characteristic is the over-simplification of is-sues, which often lead to a naive polarisation. The debate about teaching methods is reduced to a choice between the didactic and the informal. (Professor Paul Black, 1992, p. 5)

In 1989 Margaret Thatcher said that she felt that Kenneth Baker's presentational flair was needed for the next election in two or three years time — or was this another ploy to get her own way in education? In any case Baker left education before he could complete the imple-mentation phase of the National Curriculum and the rest of his policies. He became Chairman of the Party.

John MacGregor July 1989 to November 1990

Baker was replaced in the July 1989 reshuffle by John MacGregor — hitherto a very low profile politician. MacGregor remained in education for little more than a year (until November 1990), but he was regarded within education as a conciliator who saw the need for a period of calm and stability. Many education professionals saw him as a consensus seeker who might repair some of the recent damage to the system. Nevertheless, MacGregor has to take some of the blame for adding to the National Curriculum confusion: in an attempt to simplify assess-ment at Key Stage 1 (age 7), he was guilty of beginning the dismantling of the TGAT National Curriculum assessment model and abandoning the principle of a broad and balanced entitlement curriculum for all.

In January 1990, speaking to the Society of Education Officers' Conference, MacGregor suggested that some pupils might be allowed to drop some National Curriculum foundation subjects at Key Stage 4 (age 14–16). Later in the year (July 1990), Duncan Graham, on behalf of the National Curriculum Council, advised against dropping foundation subjects, but his advice was not taken: MacGregor replied with the government view that all pupils would be required to follow the three core subjects (English, maths and science) to 16, together with a modern language and technology (the extended core), but for the rest of the foundation subjects there should be 'flexibility'. This was a serious departure from the Kenneth Baker ideal of an entitlement curriculum for all 5–16 which was already a watered-down version of the HMI model of entitlement.

Meanwhile, in July 1990 there had been a reshuffle and Junior Ministers Angela Rumbold and Robert Jackson were replaced by two right wingers, Tim Eggar and Michael Fallon (a member of the 'No Turning Back' group which had advocated the privatization of schools).

After MacGregor had been in office for a year, education became the 'big idea' of the year, especially at the annual conference: the Conservatives wanted to use education as the major political issue of 1990 (despite the fact — or maybe because of the fact — that this was the year of the Gulf War and the decision to take Britain into the Exchange Rate Mechanism). But John MacGregor's conference speech on education was a disappointment and was criticized by many of his colleagues. Ten days later he had a formal meeting with the Prime Minister which at first was interpreted as an occasion when the Education Secretary had gained Thatcher's support for the policy of simplifying testing at age 7, but a few weeks later MacGregor was replaced by Kenneth Clarke. In her memoirs Margaret Thatcher (1993) says she replaced MacGregor because she realized that he was not presenting the Conservative education policies sufficiently well (p. 835).

Many regretted MacGregor's departure because he had gained the reputation of being a good listener. He seems to have been a pluralist who was nevertheless driven along in the direction of the right-wing privatizers, still a very strident and powerful minority within the Party, supported frequently by Margaret Thatcher herself. But his later performance as Secretary of State for Transport in 1993 when he stuck to a very unpopular policy of rail privatization may well indicate that he was not unsympathetic to some of the market ideas in education. He was another Secretary of State who failed to see the incompatibility of a pluralist position in education and the privatizers' doctrine of unrestrained choice. His behaviour in Education and elsewhere lends support to the Marquand thesis (see chapter 4) that by 1988 there were no 'wets' in the Cabinet; in my terms even pluralists like MacGregor were now using the language and ideas of the privatizers. In this respect, he may be taken as a typical 'Tory Mind' of the 1989–90 vintage.

During the Summer of 1990, the need for a new initiative in education had been underlined by the Presidential Address of Sir Claus Moser at the annual meeting of the British Association. Moser, a distinguished academic, one of whose previous posts had been head of government statistics, was a voice that should not have been ignored. But it was. He criticized the quality of the education service, called for greatly increased resources and complained that the British were among the most poorly educated in the Western world. He urged the Prime Minister to set up a Royal Commission on Education. This idea was immediately rejected as unnecessary, but the notion of a thorough independent review was taken up in the form of the National Commission on Education which was funded by the Paul Hamlyn Foundation (see chapter 7 below).

MacGregor made few contributions in his speeches to education policy; he seemed to see his role as making a changing system work and to simplify it rather than to introduce new ideas. Shortly after he had left Education, he made a speech at University College, Swansea, sharing the platform with James (now Lord) Callaghan, who fifteen years before had initiated the 'Great Debate' on education. The idea was to continue the debate started in 1976. MacGregor's speech consisted largely of some good-natured Party-political sparring with Callaghan, but it did throw some light on Tory attitudes to education in 1991. Firstly, MacGregor justified the emphasis that he, as Education Secretary, had put on the functional aspects of education and the need to improve relations between industry and education. In this context he confessed that he had been impressed by reading Correlli Barnett's *Audit of War* (one of the books Keith Joseph had told his civil servants to read) and Martin Wiener's *English Culture and the Decline of the Industrial Spirit 1850–1980.* (In chapter 3 I made some reference to Margaret Thatcher commenting on Keith Joseph's similar concern about the 'anti-enterprise' culture at the DES.) MacGregor clearly believed that Tory policies had begun to rectify that situation. He also believed that the National Curriculum was already improving standards (and he tried to justify his own action in slimming down the National Curriculum Key Stage 4). He used the standards issue as an opportunity to question child-centred learning which he also linked with 'too much emphasis on coursework'! In that context, too, he followed the Party line in wanting to retain 'A' Levels but encouraging a separate, less academic, route from the age of 16 to 18. Finally, he was somewhat critical of HMI. He concluded by expressing his approval for a few more Conservative policies — parental choice, City Technology Colleges and the expansion of higher education (including 'the freeing of polytechnics from the LEAs'). At heart a pluralist Tory Mind but confused by the privatizers' language of choice and the market.

Kenneth Clarke, November 1990 to April 1992

MacGregor was replaced by Kenneth Clarke on 2 November 1990, who, it was said, only reluctantly agreed to transfer his skills from the National Health Service to Education. Clarke was in office from November 1990 to April 1992, thus having the unique distinction of serving as Education Secretary to both Thatcher and Major. Within a month he had announced that from the Summer of 1991 all school-leavers would take with them a record of achievement. This was generally welcomed by teachers and employers, but another statement later in the month was less acceptable. Clarke declared that in order to help parents make an informed choice of school, all schools would be required to produce examination results in a standard form so that league tables could be published. Another example of a pluralist who was now using the language and ideas of the privatizers — choice and the market.

In other respects Kenneth Clarke displayed Tory credentials in the form of exaggerated respect for cultural heritage — especially in his negotiations over the National Curriculum for history and he insisted that history should not be confused with current affairs; he was also against any kind of mixing of subjects, in the form of humanities, for example.

22 November 1990: from Thatcher to Major; from 'Victorian Values' to 'Back to Basics'

The details of the events leading to the fall of Margaret Thatcher need not concern us here. Her replacement by John Major was less a matter of ideology than of personal style and political survival. She had been increasingly dictatorial in her dealings with Cabinet Ministers and this was combined with her growing unpopularity with the electorate, not least caused by her obsessive attachment to the unpopular Poll Tax. In addition, her behaviour on Europe was causing great concern both within the Parliamentary Party and inside the Cabinet.

Before moving on to the Major era, however, it is important to comment briefly on another of Margaret Thatcher's *bêtes noires*: teacher training. Throughout her period as Prime Minister, Mrs Thatcher was obsessed by the need to reform teacher education and training. She had shared with Keith Joseph the idea that teacher training institutions were centres of progressivist theory which produced ineffective teachers, and Joseph had set up the Council for the Accreditation of Teacher Education (CATE) in 1984. The Prime Minister had also instructed Kenneth Baker to follow this up with 'more reforms'; he obliged with two schemes — Licensed Teachers and Articled Teachers. The Licensed Teachers Scheme was designed to attract those who might want to enter teaching as a second career; the Articled Teacher idea was, in Margaret Thatcher's own words, 'essentially an apprenticeship scheme of "on-the-job" training for younger graduates'.

As we shall see later in this chapter, Thatcher's teacher training policies were to continue unchanged under Major: Clarke and Patten both continued with this negative aspect of the Tory Mind and pushed through 'anti-theory' policies sometimes in the face of considerable opposition. This feature of Thatcherism — extreme hostility towards education theory and teacher education — clearly became part of the Tory Mind in the 1990s: at the 1992 Conservative Party Conference, John Major said: 'I also want reform of teacher training. Let us return to basic subject teaching, not courses in the theory of education. Primary teachers should learn how to teach children to read, not waste their time on the politics of gender, race and class.'

The real question for education was whether Thatcher being replaced by Major would make any ideological difference. Nigel Lawson in his memoirs suggests that none of the three contenders for the leadership of the Party (Heseltine, Hurd and Major) was a Thatcherite. But what united the Party was a common desire to make sure that the Labour Party did not win the next General Election. For the moment ideology mattered less than victory. John Major seemed to be the candidate most likely to unite the Party and successfully woo the voters in time to avoid a Labour government in 1992.

What difference has John Major as Prime Minister made in terms of ideology? He began by making statements about his desire for a 'classless society' which although sounding strange from any Tory Prime Minister (see chapter 6), gave some moderates reason for hoping that Thatcherite policies — including those in education — would be softened or even eliminated. As we shall see, these were false hopes.

Meanwhile, continuing at the DES, Kenneth Clarke was pursuing policies very much in the tradition of the Thatcher years. His first real test came in January 1991 when he addressed his first North of England Conference (in Leeds). He said that one of his aims was greater *choice and diversity* (a slogan that was to be the title of his successor's White Paper). He then made a statement which seemed excessive to many of those present:

> Education must become irreversibly dominated by the needs of pupils and their parents. It must offer a variety of provision to enable choice to be made to meet a variety of needs and preferences. Monolithic uniformity is the curse of giant public services . . . (DES 2/91, 4 January 1991)

He said that imposing all ten subjects as well as Religious Education would leave insufficient time for the 'sensible choices which 14 year olds and their parents must be entitled to consider'. His solution was to move further away from the Baker planned entitlement curriculum for the 14–16 age group; at Key Stage 4 he inclined towards 'more flexibility and choice' in the form of a new five-tier hierarchy of subjects:

1 Core subjects (all students would take GCSE in English, maths and science).
2 Extended core (all would take technology and a modern language but not necessarily GCSE).
3 History *or* geography (all would *choose* either history or geography or a mixture).
4 Art and music become completely optional (more flexibility, more choice).
5 PE (all must do PE but there would be 'a particularly flexible definition of PE').

From her memoirs we know that this was part of a policy that had been favoured by Margaret Thatcher; although she had ceased to be Prime Minister, many of her views on education had been accepted by most of the Conservative Party.

Clarke went on to say that he would also be encouraging the vocational examining bodies to develop pre-vocational qualifications for 16 year olds certifying attainment in the whole or parts of foundation subjects, thus competing with the existing GCSE Groups. He also wanted them to develop qualifications covering other studies outside the National Curriculum 'for those pupils . . . likely to want a curriculum at 14 and 15 which has a distinctly pre-vocational character'. A new form of Tory selection was creeping in at the age of 14.

Clarke also announced that the attainment targets in maths and science would have to be reduced because he had been advised that the GCSE examining groups found them incompatible with their existing grading systems and could not guarantee continuity of standards in 1994 (when it was intended to harmonize the TGAT ten levels with the GCSE grading system). To the North of England Conference this sounded perilously close to the curriculum being dominated by assessment — something which has always been condemned by educationists but is less offensive to Tory politicians.

In the same speech, Clarke announced that schools would be pushed even further in the direction of 'open enrolment' — that is, allowing parents the right to *choose* a school as long as there was space available. Another example of giving individual choice for a minority higher priority than a planned system for all. Two days later, Clarke again demonstrated his Thatcherite credentials by praising 'A' Levels but expressing scepticism about the 'core skills' concept. He was clearly a person — not uncommon among Tories — who liked curriculum knowledge kept in neat subject packages. He later made it known to the National Curriculum Council (NCC) that he wanted to hear no more about core skills or any other 'cross-curricular' areas, themes or skills — another view that the supposedly 'left-wing' Clarke shared with Margaret Thatcher on the other side of the Party.

In January 1991 Clarke issued a press release, without prior warning to the GCSE groups, stating that for the 1991 papers examiners would have to deduct up to 5 per cent of marks for errors in spelling. The Groups patiently explained why more notice would be needed. He continued to show his respect for these professionals by asking the GCSE groups to take on the task of 'auditing' the Key Stage 3 National Curriculum assessment — but without the 'full paraphernalia' of external marking and moderating.

In February 1991 the Prime Minister showed that he was taking a personal direct interest in education: he told the Young Conservatives that he wanted to see more vocational courses in schools; a few weeks later, Clarke returned to another aspect of the same theme: he said that the 'A' Level and NVQ routes should be equally valued (although 'A' Level was still the Gold Standard). In another speech (to a Conservative Party Local Government Conference in February 1991) Clarke said he had no intention of restoring grammar schools but choice and competition were necessary to raise standards.

In May 1991, Clarke found another enemy within the educational establishment — HMI. As we have seen, Margaret Thatcher, Kenneth Baker and John MacGregor were all variously critical of HMI as part of the 'producer' establishment. Clarke announced that HMI would be reviewed — yet again. The eventual dismemberment of HMI and conversion into OFSTED and privatized inspection teams, was presumably caused by a mixture of irritation with independent views within the central authority and the ideological imperative that whenever possible public services should be privatized. The influence of the Right was quite clear on this issue — soon after Clarke's announcement of a review, the two former Junior Ministers, Bob Dunn and Rhodes Boyson, put down a Private Members Bill proposing the complete abolition of HMI. Experts are unnecessary when the market takes over.

In June 1991, Clarke delivered the Westminster Lecture. This lecture shows, at a crucial moment in the history of the Party, how the ideology established during the Thatcher years was not only still alive but still developing. He began by contrasting 'Conservative belief in choice and competition' with 'the monolithic statism of the left' — very much the language of Keith Joseph and the Centre for Policy Studies. But Clarke now related that 'philosophy' to John Major's notion of a 'classless society' — which might more accurately be called a meritocratic society. Clarke seemed to believe that comprehensive schools were an obstacle to that kind of society, as were the 'progressive' views of expert educationists which he dismissed as 'left wing'. He implied that given freedom, schools would reject the modern ideas on teaching methods and class management. He thought that the National Curriculum would also help because it 'challenges those theories and sets out programmes of study which require organized teaching of facts and of skills which all the inhabitants of the classless society will need to command in the modern world'. He then proceeded to attack the ideas of Rousseau and Dewey (leaning heavily on the right-wing Professor Anthony O'Hear, but without acknowledgment).

He continued with that anti-expert policy in the Summer of 1991 when in the course of one week in July he dismissed (or caused the resignation of) the Chairmen and Chief Executives of both the National Curriculum Council (NCC) and the School Examinations and Assessment Council (SEAC). Duncan Graham (NCC) and Philip Halsey (SEAC) gave him advice about the National Curriculum and its assessment which he found unacceptable. They were replaced by the non-expert but more politically acceptable right wingers — David Pascall and Brian Griffiths, both of whom had served in Margaret Thatcher's Policy Unit — Lord Griffiths as its loyal Head for many years. (In his memoirs, Nigel Lawson said Griffiths only told the Prime Minister what she wanted to know.)

In July 1991, John Major, for the first time, made a speech entirely devoted to education — to the right-wing think-tank, the Centre for Policy Studies (CPS). It was similar in content and style to the speeches of Kenneth Clarke — clearly bidding for right-wing support. I will return to an analysis of this speech at the end of this chapter, when I recommend that anyone interested in this subject should read *Education and Mr Major* by Fred Jarvis (1993). Jarvis seized upon wild accusations about teachers and LEAs in the speech, and asked — in vain — for evidence to support them.

Having dispensed with a number of experts and in May having 'freed' the Polytechnics from LEA control (by now a standard Tory attitude), in September Clarke proceeded to put even more reliance on the market: he launched the 'Parents' Charter' requiring LEAs to produce league tables so that parents could compare schools. John Major continued to involve himself in education and played to the right-wing gallery at the Party Conference, expressing his belief in basics, and saying that 'progressive educators have had their day'. (The SEAC had been instructed not to issue any press releases during the Conference time so that such wisdom would get full press coverage.)

In January 1992 Clarke continued with the reform of teacher education. Once again he chose the North of England Conference to make his intentions known. In his Southport speech (4 January 1992) Clarke said he wanted trainee secondary teachers to spend twice as much time in schools (with less time available for theory) — another favourite idea of Margaret Thatcher. He liked the notion of 'mentor' teachers in the context of partner schools and school-based training. He was also attracted to the idea of criteria as 'statements of competence' as a way of designing new courses for training teachers. In other words, he was accepting the behavioural objectives model of curriculum planning which is, ironically, the most theoretical of all approaches to course design. (By this time it was, however, known that two senior civil servants in the DFE had tried to persuade Clarke that his plans were expensive and unworkable, and had been moved to other duties for their pains.) This speech was interesting for a number of reasons. Clarke was clearly in favour of less theory but more practical training (the apprenticeship model that Margaret Thatcher had referred to). He was also demonstrating his preference for simple tests in terms of outcomes rather than more sophisticated measures. Tories sometimes appear to prefer training to education.

Clarke is an interesting example of the Tory Mind in other ways. Margaret Thatcher in her memoirs referred to him as on the left wing of the Party; he had previously been a pluralist much in favour of state education; yet now he too was apparently won over to the use of privatizing language — 'choice' dominated his policies on the National Curriculum and assessment. He was also consistently anti-theory, condemning the 'standard assessment tasks' in 1991 as 'elaborate nonsense', preferring paper and pencil tests he had been advised were unreliable. For example, on 2 January 1992, the National Association of Head Teachers had sent him a list of serious flaws in Key Stage 1 assessment and this was reinforced by Professor Desforges at the North of England Conference. He was also unwilling to trust the teachers on such matters as course work. In January 1992 he said that 'A'-Level course work should be restricted as in the 'reformed' GCSE, despite expert views available — for example, in the TES for 3 January 1992 Duncan Graham regretted the lack of 'informed debate' on the relative merits of course work and traditional examinations. (The total percentage of marks achievable by course work in GCSE subjects had been reduced to 20–30 per cent in 1991 on the orders of Kenneth Clarke.)

More than any other Education Secretary hitherto, Clarke was willing to intervene personally on matters concerning teaching method and the content of the curriculum: there was a prolonged row between politicians and experts on both art and music where Clarke wanted to give priority to 'knowledge' over 'performance'. The eminent conductor, Simon Rattle, criticized the revised proposals for National Curriculum music as 'a return to the passive history and appreciation teaching of 30 years ago'. (See Lawson, Plummeridge and Swanwick, 1993, for a detailed discussion of the dispute.) It was also Clarke who ruled that history ended twenty years ago.

Clarke even supported those clauses in the Education (Schools) Bill (1992) which not only privatized the schools' inspections, but also allowed schools to *choose* their own inspecting teams. (That part of the Bill was eventually modified partly as a result of Lord Beloff and other Conservative peers in the House of Lords — but the privatization of inspections continued, together with the dismantling of Her Majesty's Inspectorate. The 450 members of HMI were reduced to a rump of about 180 to supervise the privatized system.) Clarke also insisted on the publication of National Curriculum assessment and examination results in league table form, despite being repeatedly told that this information was both misleading and unfair to the schools. He must have understood the arguments but acted as though the league table principle was an essential feature of education policy.

Clarke continued to be unpopular with teachers and other professionals up to the 1992 General Election. He survived, but one of his Junior Ministers, Michael Fallon, lost his seat. In the post-Election reshuffle, Clarke was promoted by John Major, to become Chancellor of the Exchequer.

John Patten April 1992 to 1994

Many breathed a sigh of relief when Clarke was replaced by John Patten in April 1992. Patten was regarded as on the left of the Party in some respects, and having been a university teacher was expected to have better than average understanding of education. He has disappointed the optimists.

Throughout 1992 and 1993 Patten was struggling to make National Curriculum assessment work, faced by the increasing hostility of teachers who objected to flawed tests and the demands made on them to administer and mark the tests. (Further details will be given later in this chapter.)

In July 1992 Eric Bolton (recently retired Senior Chief Inspector), in a speech to the Council of Local Education Authorities, criticized the government, including Patten, for paying too much attention to right-wing pressure groups.

Sadly, despite the rhetoric of Citizens and Parents Charters, the Government shows little sign of being a listening Government. When it does, it listens so selectively that most of those in the education service fear that what they have to say falls on deaf ears. The Government does not seem to listen to

1. Heads and teachers; teacher associations; governors and education researchers, on the difficult issues of school effectiveness, value-added and league tables. It *does* listen to John Marks and the Adam Smith Institute.

2. Heads of schools; governing bodies; head teacher associations; Vice-Chancellors and teacher trainers, when it sets out to reform teacher training. It *does* listen to Sheila Lawlor whose critique of Initial Teacher Training is based on a somewhat selective reading of course prospectuses and is not complicated by ever having visited and systematically observed what goes on.

3. Public examination boards; chief examiners; most heads and teachers; HMI and large employers, when it sets out to squeeze the GCSE back into a GCE 'O' Level mould. It *does* listen to the Centre for Policy Studies and a small group of independent school heads.

4. HMI; heads of effective primary schools, and non-ideologically driven experts on the teaching of reading. It *does* listen to Martin Turner who initially claimed, on somewhat elusive evidence, that reading standards in England were falling across the board (not true) and that *the cause* was that primary schools had rushed, or been led, wholesale into modern, trendy teaching of reading based on the 'Real Books' approach (again not true). There is no crime in listening to your political friends. But a wise government listens more widely than that, and especially to those with no political axe to grind. It is not auspicious that the formal channels of advice about education to the Government appear to be either muzzled (e.g. HMI), or packed with people likely to say whatever the Government wants to hear (i.e. the NCC and SEAC). ('Imaginary Gardens with Real Toads' in Chitty and Simon, 1993, p. 15)

In August 1992, at the British Association Annual Conference, Professor Paul Black, President of the Education Section, complained that the National Curriculum and assessment system should have been accompanied by a research programme but research projects proposed by the NCC had been blocked by successive Ministers. Worse still, the curriculum had been subjected to a series of unnecessary changes in the course of implementation. Teachers who were originally compliant had become hostile. Valid and effective assessment procedures had been replaced by unreliable short tests. Black too was critical of the government's willingness to listen to right-wing pressure groups (especially the CPS) rather than expert advice. Lady Blatch said that Professor Black, who in 1987 had been chosen by government to chair the Task Group for Assessment and Testing (TGAT), was out of touch. A few weeks later, Professor Brian Cox, editor of the Black Papers, and hitherto a supporter of government education reforms, became critical of government policy. In his autobiography, *The Great Betrayal* (published in September 1992), he accused the government of sacrificing the National Curriculum for English to right-wing prejudices within the Conservative Party. He also suggested that right wingers had been given to understand that if they toed the line on Europe, their voice would be heard on education.

The government seemed to be in danger of antagonizing not only the teaching profession but even those right of centre who had previously been supporters of Conservative reforms — for example the Headmasters' Conference (HMC) representing the views of prestigious independent schools. The reason for widespread opposition to government policies on education included a series of discernible ideological shifts: assessment methods which were increasingly unprofessional; changes to the English curriculum; the tendency to try to control teaching methods as well as the curriculum. Even Sir Malcolm Thornton, the Conservative Chairman of the House of Commons Select Committee on Education, in a speech at De Montfort University (3 December 1992), complained about the government being unduly influenced by right-wing pressure groups whom he referred to as 'lords of misrule' and purveyors of 'insidious propaganda'.

> If only we could have drawn breath after the passing of the 1988 Act. There was a brief moment — under the charge of John MacGregor — when it looked as though that might happen. But that glimmer of light was snuffed out before most people realised it was there! From that point on, I believe that both the wider debate and the ears of Ministers have been disproportionately influenced by extremists — extremists whose pronouncements become ever wilder and further from the reality of the world of education which I recognise, in which I work and for which I care deeply. And who are they to foist upon the children of this country ideas which will only serve to take them backwards? What hard evidence do they have to support their assertions? How often do they actually go into schools and see for themselves what is really happening? What possible authority can they claim for representing the views of the overwhelming majority of parents? (In Chitty and Simon, 1993, pp. 172–73)

Patten had two unfortunate characteristics: first, he wanted to convince the right wing that he was not a wet; second, like several of his predecessors, he felt that he knew the answers (simple answers to complex questions), refused to listen to professional advice and pushed on with misguided policies despite almost unanimous opposition. His White Paper *Choice and Diversity* (1992) became known in the DFE as 'Chaos and Perversity'. He was proud of having written some of the sections himself. It was extremely long and was criticized for lacking coherence, but it formed the basis of the 1993 Education Act. Patten's eventual claim to fame may be that he produced an Education Act (1993) even longer than Baker's ERA (1988). The fact that so complex a piece of legislation was apparently needed so soon after the 1988 Act was itself an indication of the confusion that was a feature of education policy in those years.

John Patten's speech at the Conservative Party Conference in 1992 was another blatant example of playing to the right wing. He, like John Major, wanted to reform teacher training. And he showed his contempt for another group of experts — the Public Examination Boards. On the basis of a very mild critical comment by HMI of some GCSE procedures, he arrogantly announced to the Tory Conference:

> Well, I have a message for those exam boards: 'Listen very carefully. I will say this only once. Get your act together!' The litany of educational let-down has gone on long enough. (Conference Press Release)

He also confirmed that he (like Margaret Thatcher but not Kenneth Baker) wanted *all* schools to become Grant Maintained and be freed from LEA control. He then rounded on the familiar scapegoat — teacher training:

> Just as we need to ensure that our children are well taught, so we need to be certain that our teachers are practically trained — not with the discredited theories of the 1960s, but as much as possible at the chalkface, in the classroom . . . I also want to extend the routes into teaching: to give greater opportunities to those who have already raised a family and have something to offer to our young school children.

He concluded by boasting of the Conservative achievements so far — including the National Curriculum with 'regular testing of all our children'.

In the Summer of 1993, because Patten refused to listen to teachers and assessment advisers, a dispute arose about the assessment of the National Curriculum — to begin with it was Key Stage 3 for English, but other subjects rapidly followed. The teachers eventually conducted a successful boycott of all the tests at Key Stages 1, 2 and 3, and a professional 'listener' had to be found in the shape of Sir Ron Dearing, who was not only appointed to be the Chairman Designate of the School Curriculum and Assessment Authority (SCAA), which was not due to start until October 1993, but who was, unprecedentedly, asked in June 1993 to take over the running of both the SEAC and the NCC immediately. The matter was clearly regarded as urgent. During the dispute about Key Stage 3 testing in 1992 and 1993, Patten had managed to quarrel with even more groups and individuals who were normally considered to be moderate or even right of centre. For example, Elizabeth Diggory, the President of the GSA (Independent Girls'

Schools) criticized Key Stage 3 tests for their emphasis on rote learning and suggested that many independent schools would not be taking part in 1993; she also criticized politicians for seeming to tell teachers how to teach. The immediate response of Lady Blatch, the Minister of State responsible, was to resort to abuse, saying that Miss Diggory's views were ridiculous and full of old 1960s arguments.

During the Summer of 1993 John Patten became ill: some alleged stress, others pleaded a virus. He was away for six weeks but, contrary to expectations, returned to resume his post at the DFE. And to resume the attack on teacher education and training. It may have been the case that the pressure for the 'reform' of teacher education was now coming from the Prime Minister (advised — via his adviser on education, Nick True — by Professor Anthony O'Hear, a Bradford University philosopher); Patten took on the task with apparent enthusiasm and the result was the 1993 Bill which was introduced immediately after the Queen's Speech in November 1993. One of the proposals in the Bill was to isolate teacher education from the rest of higher education, handing over the funding and approval of courses, and research to a new quango — the Teacher Training Agency (TTA). Unusually, the Bill was discussed first in the House of Lords where it was greatly criticized. The Conservative peer, Lord Beloff, was quoted as saying 'The Secretary of State will probably appoint another lot of businessmen of whom the President of the Board of Trade says only 2 per cent are any good. The only people who don't realize this are in the DFE.' Some other Conservative peers were equally critical. For example, the Earl of Limerick said:

> ... the argument for a separate training agency seems strange and, it might be said, perverse. What then is the rationale for distancing teacher training from higher education, where logic would seem to place it? Surely there must be extra costs involved. Further, what precedents do we signal from that intention? today it is teachers; tomorrow, will it be lawyers, engineers ... or what? The signal for higher education is not a positive one. (Hansard, 7 December 1993)

Very few supporters could be found for the Bill, but Patten insisted on continuing with it. At the time of writing (March 1994) John Patten was still in post — to the surprise of some, but explained by others as an Education Secretary who could be relied upon to go along with Major's educational priorities — 'back to basics'. At a conference in Oxford in January 1994, John Patten had succeeded in converting that slogan (which had become something of a joke) into an action programme for education. He called on schools to improve their teaching of values and provided them with a list of core values:

> Self-reliance and self-discipline;
> acceptance of responsibility;
> regard for proper authority;
> unselfishness and the need for self-restraint;
> dignity, courtesy and respect for oneself and for others;
> sensitivity towards the needs and views of others;
> fairness;
> honesty and trustworthiness;
> loyalty and fidelity;
> the readiness to stand up for what one believes in;
> the capacity to look to the future as well as relishing the present and absorbing the lessons of the past. (Patten to the Oxford Conference, 5 January 1994)

It was reported that many of the teachers in the audience felt that they were already doing their best in this sphere and that the list simply told them what they already knew. The last item on the list, however, might be an excellent starting point for a reformed Conservative Party.

Meanwhile, the Dearing Final Report (January 1994) had for the moment relieved the pressure on Patten, but the cost had been considerable in curriculum terms. Part of the Dearing solution (which was immediately accepted by Government) was that the National Curriculum would effectively cease at 14: most teachers were interested in 'streamlining the national curriculum', but many of the long-term problems of detail in the national curriculum and its assessment remained unsolved.

Epilogue to chapter 5: the Jarvis–Major Correspondence

Earlier in the chapter I referred briefly to this correspondence, but I wanted to leave space for a more detailed analysis of this evidence — as an indicator of the state of the Tory Mind on education from 1991 onwards. I will not attempt to follow the whole story chronologically: it would be much better for everyone to read the original text (Jarvis, 1993), but I would like to focus on a few important issues that arose from the correspondence.

Jarvis began, on 16 July 1991, by writing to John Major about his speech, 'Education — All Our Futures', to the Centre for Policy Studies (CPS) on 3 July 1991. In that speech the Prime Minister had made some sweeping criticisms of teachers and the education service — without providing any evidence. Fred Jarvis (who had been General Secretary of the NUT from 1975 to 1989) asked him to put this right:

> If education and training are now to loom large as election issues, I hope you will agree that the debate on them should be based on fact, not fiction, and that politicians should present evidence to substantiate their assertions about what is happening in our schools and colleges.
>
> Regrettably, in my opinion, your recent speech to the CPS failed to meet those tests. If you think this unfair I invite you to provide the evidence on which you based the following points in your speech:
>
> (1) You allege that there was 'a mania that condemns children to fall short of their potential; that treated them as if they were identical or must be made so. A mania that undermined common sense values in schools, rejected proven teaching methods, debased standards — or disposed of them altogether.'
>
> I share your view that it is the task of the educator to develop each child's potential to the full and that teacher expectations are a vital factor in what children achieve. But when you say you cannot forgive 'the Left' for depriving 'great cohorts of our children of the opportunities they deserve' you must be aware that by implication you are accusing large numbers of teachers of responsibility for the situation you describe. What is your evidence for such a serious change? And given that we have had Conservative Governments for most of the period you were referring to, do you apportion any blame to your own Party?
>
> (2) You claim that the Government has been engaged in 'a struggle to resist the insidious attacks on literature and history in our schools'. Who has been making those attacks and how widespread are they? What has HMI reported on those matters?
>
> (3) You state that 'there are city education authorities employing more bureaucrats than teachers'. Chris Patten made a similar charge some time ago. It is, I believe, a falsehood, one which I am surprised somebody in your position should utter. Can you name the education authorities guilty of that practice? (p. 14)

There were other questions in the letter but those three quoted above will illustrate the point I want to make. The correspondence continued until the 15 February 1993 when Fred Jarvis understandably gave up. Most of the 'replies' came from staff at the Prime Minister's office, but on 17 February and 25 June 1992, John Major signed replies himself. They were no more satisfactory than those from his political staff (except that he apologized for his office not dealing with the original letter properly — 'there is no excuse for such sloppiness').

I want to make just three points: firstly, there was a complete failure to mount any intellectually respectable argument in defence of Major's CPS lecture by providing evidence of any kind to support his sweeping generalizations or specific accusations. Jarvis complains about the Prime Minister's resorting to platitudes and clichés rather than evidence and argument. Secondly, extreme right-wing views influenced John Major's thinking about education. Jarvis points out in his commentary that not only was his first speech on education given to the CPS, but that Major chose to deliver a second speech to the equally right-wing Adam Smith Institute (16 June 1992). In addition, the content of the 'replies' is full of familiar right-wing prejudices. One long letter contains an attack on Rousseau and Dewey (neither of whom was mentioned by Jarvis) which was taken, as Jarvis points out (p. 7), almost word for word from a pamphlet by the right-wing polemicist Anthony O'Hear. Jarvis observed that John Major has never attempted to challenge the ideologues in the way that other Conservatives like Edward Heath and Malcolm Thornton have. Lastly, the No. 10 staff were incompetent in their dealings with Jarvis's straightforward enquiries. (On 15 January 1992 Judith Chaplin apologized for one of her colleagues' 'gross incompetence' and John Major repeated the apology on 17 February 1992.) At a time when education was a top priority for the Party, it seemed strange that they clearly had difficulty in finding someone to reply who knew anything about it. This incompetence is symptomatic of a failure to take education seriously and trying to treat it as 'common sense'. Jarvis refers to 'distorted perception and warped vision': that sounds a reasonable description not just of John Major but of the Tory Mind on education in the 1990s.

Chapter 6

Ideology and Policies 1979–94: Some Problems and Contradictions

> Thatcherism is based on a simplistic view of human nature, which reflects more the qualities of the ideologist than any common attributes of mankind. The Thatcherite theory is unusually unconvincing, however, since it manages to be both too pessimistic and too optimistic. It is too pessimistic, in that it assumes that everyone is driven by selfish motives; it is too optimistic, in that it asserts that everyone pursues his selfish interests in a rational manner. (Sir Ian Gilmour, 1992, p. 271)

In earlier chapters I have concentrated mainly on what Conservatives have said and written about education during the period 1979–94. In this chapter I want to switch the emphasis to what they did — particularly the legislation they passed. The chapter is divided into two sections: in the first I will briefly review Conservative education policies which have been transformed into legislation, more or less in chronological order, with a view to relating policies to Tory dogmatics and especially to ideological changes over the fifteen-year period. Each piece of legislation will be described briefly and linked to six ideological 'key words'. In the second part of the chapter, those six key words will be analyzed and discussed. Finally, the key words will be related to problems and contradictions in Tory thought and practice in education.

Codd (1988) has suggested that the analysis of policy documents is a difficult task and warns against simply accepting policy statements as expressions of political purpose — intentions may be different from statements of intent. I have no problem with accepting those distinctions and I hope I have consistently avoided such dangers in earlier chapters — although I would not wish to travel all the way down that road to post-modernism. It is partly for the reasons that Codd has drawn our attention to that I now wish to concentrate on what the Conservative Party has decided to make into *law*, without ignoring the rhetoric behind the legislation.

The Legislation

The 1979 Education Act

The first, entirely predictable, education legislation for the Thatcher government was the 1979 Act which fulfilled the promise of reversing the previous administration's decision to require all LEAs to move towards a complete system of comprehensive secondary schooling: the Labour Party's 1976 Act was repealed. For at least fifteen years the issue of comprehensive secondary schools had been the most frequent educational topic for debate at party conferences and elsewhere. It was an interesting example of ideology because abandoning comprehensive schools did not have universal popular appeal: several Conservative controlled LEAs had tried to reverse comprehensive plans and reintroduce selective schools, but this had been resisted by voters, including Tory voters. The politicians, as might be expected, were more ideologically committed to selection than the rank and file. Thus the 1979 Act merely removed the compulsory requirement to have a comprehensive system: it did nothing to enforce decomprehensivization. More subtle approaches to achieve that end would be adopted later.

Key word: selection

The 1980 Education Act

The 1980 Act was much more wide-ranging, but most of the items covered were concerned with extending parents' choice: the Assisted Places Scheme (APS); more parents on governing bodies; LEAs and governors required to provide information for parents; the restriction of the LEA right to refuse places to those outside their area. In addition, independent schools were to be registered; and greater control was to be exerted over the Advanced Further Education pool.

The Assisted Places Scheme subsidized places in some independent schools for 'academic' pupils whose parents could not afford to pay the full fees. Unfortunately, this provision inevitably had the effect of signalling to parents that their local comprehensive schools were not appropriate for bright children. Parents' rights were increased in several ways. But 'what winners win, losers lose'. Local education authorities were destined to be the losers from 1979 onwards. The more power parents are given in choosing, the more restricted is the LEAs' ability to plan. Similarly, with the clauses dealing with Advanced Further Education, further restrictions were imposed upon LEA planning.

Key words: centralization, expenditure, choice/market

The 1981 Education Act

The Warnock Report (1978) during the Callaghan administration had made wide-ranging recommendations about the education of children with special needs. Some, but not all, of the Warnock recommendations were addressed by this Act which made LEAs responsible for providing suitable services for such children, and gave parents increased rights to challenge LEA decisions. It seemed to some critics that LEAs were being given additional responsibilities without any more power or resources.

Key word: choice

The 1983 White Paper: Teaching Quality

The publication of *Teaching Quality* was one stage in the complex process of the DES/DFE engineering more control over the crucial area of teacher education (see chapter 5 for more details). Following this publication, the Committee for the Accreditation of Teacher Education (CATE) was set up in 1984 'to advise the Secretaries of State for Education on the approval of initial teacher training courses'. Unless courses were approved they did not carry qualified teacher status. In order to be recommended for approval by CATE, courses had to have been inspected by HMI and be seen to comply with a number of criteria (known as the 'CATE criteria' although they were established by the Secretary of State).

Key words: expert/theory, centralization

The 1984 Education (Grants and Awards) Act

This legislation enabled the DES to offer grants to LEAs for a selected list of specific DES priorities. Since there was no 'new money', in effect the Act gave the DES more control over local spending.

Key words: centralization, expenditure

The 1985 White Paper: Better Schools

This White Paper is described by Knight (1990) as 'a kind of modern Black Paper'. In justification of this seemingly harsh judgment, Knight quotes a briefing paper for Tory MPs from the Conservative Research Department Education Desk Officer:

> The present government is determined to undo the damage caused by the misconceptions of the 1960s. A series of policies is being painstakingly developed and gradually implemented — policies necessarily using many different instruments, but unusually coherent in their approach and with the potential to bring about a restoration of a common-sense approach to education in place of Labour's dogma.

Key words: traditional methods

The 1986 Education Act

The 1986 Act, which was concerned with the LEA Training Grants Scheme (LEATGS), carried on the tradition from the 1984 legislation: more power to the centre; less autonomy for LEAs. It is quite clear from the memoirs of Nigel Lawson and those of Margaret Thatcher that LEAs were a prime target — partly for purely financial reasons, partly for political control.

Key words: centralization, expenditure

The 1986 Education (No. 2) Act

This Act gave additional powers to school governors over their schools' finances. Every school was now required to have a separate governing body; the formula for representation included a stronger parental voice, governors had to present annual reports to parents and hold a meeting to discuss the report. Governors were also given the responsibility for policies on sex education, the curriculum and the prevention of political indoctrination. The powers of LEAs continued to be diminished.

Key words: centralization, expenditure

The 1987 Teachers' Pay and Conditions Act

This Act was preceded by a long dispute with the teachers about the pay award. The dispute started in early 1985 and continued until March 1986, with sporadic outbursts of one-day strikes and other actions during 1987. The Act abolished the Burnham machinery for arriving at salary awards (essentially an LEA device) and replaced it by machinery which gave the Secretary of State more direct control over teachers' pay and conditions. Conservatives had long been dissatisfied with negotiating machinery which gave central government responsibility for paying the bill without complete power to decide what the bill should be. (Nigel Lawson in his memoirs was very concerned about this.)

Key words: centralization, expenditure

The 1988 Education Reform Act

The Act (see chapter 4 for details) is interesting because it faces two ways ideologically: the clauses dealing with open enrolment, local management of schools, Grant Maintained Schools and City Technology Colleges are all concerned with increasing parental choice and encouraging schools towards market competition; on the other hand, the sections dealing with Higher and Further Education, and the ILEA increased central control. The National Curriculum was 'centralizing' in the control it exerted, but was also a market device — providing data for parental choice. The overall result of the Act was to give the Secretary of State for Education over 400 new powers (more than any other Member of the Cabinet). The Act completely changed the balance of power and influence in education.

Key words: choice, centralization

The 1990 Education Act

This Act made it possible to introduce a loans scheme for university students. For some time it had been acknowledged by most of those concerned with universities that if Higher Education was to be expanded to any significant extent then loans would have to be used to supplement or replace student grants. For additional reasons of the market, Conservatives were attracted by the notion of 'user pays' and when Keith Joseph was Education Secretary he had failed in an attempt to increase contributions from those parents who could afford to pay. The main objection to the scheme that was introduced in 1990 was that it was ideologically based: apparently Margaret Thatcher herself had vetoed any scheme which would recover the loan through national insurance or income tax contributions (for example, a graduate tax on the Australian model) — 'private enterprise' was preferred. However, after some preliminary interest, the commercial banks pulled out of the scheme leaving an expensive 'private' system to be paid for by tax payers.

Key word: expenditure

The 1992 Education (Schools) Act

A new system of privatized school inspections was introduced (see chapter 5). The Bill was rushed through in March just before the April 1992 General Election, without it being made clear how the new system would work. But part of the plan was to reduce the number of HMI from nearly 500 to 175. They would be responsible for supervising privatized teams of inspectors. The idea that schools would be able to choose their own inspection team was amended in the Lords.

Key words: expenditure, theory/experts

The 1992 Further and Higher Education Act

This Act was also approved just before the April 1992 General Election. It changed the pattern of post-16 education by removing 6th Form Colleges, tertiary and Further Education Colleges from LEA control. The financial control would be exercised by government through the Further Education Funding Councils. The Act also abolished the binary divide and allowed Polytechnics to be called Universities, financed through the Higher Education Funding Council. During discussions of the Bill, there was a good deal of comment in Parliament on the need to safeguard academic freedom, which seemed to be threatened by some provisions of the Act.

Key words: centralization, expenditure

The 1993 Education Act

This Act had been greatly discussed in its earlier form — the White Paper: *Choice and Diversity*. Parts of it were written by Education Secretary John Patten himself. It was mainly concerned with making it easier for schools to opt out of LEA control by applying for Grant Maintained status (now called 'Self-Governing Schools'). It also legislated for a new kind of school: Technology Colleges, outside LEA control. The Act also spelt out some of the measures to deal with schools regarded as 'failing' after OFSTED inspections. Such schools have to prepare 'action plans' immediately after the inspection, but if the Secretary of State considers them unsatisfactory, he can appoint an Education Association (EA). An EA has to consist of at least five people 'including at least one with direct knowledge and experience of the provision of education'. (So what do the other four know?) A school given the EA treatment either becomes 'self-governing', or, if still failing, is closed down.

Key words: centralization, choice

The 1993 Education Bill (Teacher Education)

A further move to control teacher education (see chapter 5). The funding for teacher education institutions would in future be removed from the Higher Education Funding Council and handed over to a Teacher Training Agency (TTA) directly appointed by the Education Secretary. By this means not only would initial teacher training courses be centrally controlled, but also in-service courses for teachers (including Higher Degrees) as well as educational research. The Bill was first introduced into the House of Lords where it was much criticized for giving yet more power to the Secretary of State.

Key words: centralization, experts/theory

Ideological Key Words

The ideological pressures behind the unprecedented spate of legislation from 1979 to 1994 (thirteen Acts of Parliament and countless Orders) have been summarized into six key words. I suggest that if we ignore some of the rhetoric of intention we can focus upon six overlapping, political value positions:

1 a desire for more *selection*;
2 a wish to return to *traditional* curricula and teaching methods;
3 a desire to reduce the influence of *experts and educational theory* by encouraging common-sense traditional practices (where market choice prevails, experts are unnecessary);
4 an appeal to parental *choice* as a means of encouraging *market* forces;
5 a wish to reduce educational *expenditure* (a very high priority from 1979 onwards);
6 a process of increased *centralization* which had the additional purpose of reducing the power and autonomy of LEAs.

One interesting observation about the six ideological tendencies, encapsulated in the key words, is that with the exception of the last one, all the others are 'backward-looking' in the sense that they are concerned with tradition rather than planning for the future. This is significant. In addition, each of these ideological pressures is problematic in some way; and some have built-in contradictions. I will deal with each key word in turn.

Ideology — Problems — Contradictions

For each of the six ideological key words I will first define the term and try to put it in the context of Tory policies; second, I will set out what I see as some of the problems associated with each key word; and finally I will point out some possible contradictions.

Key word 1: Selection

I have shown throughout this book that the Conservative desire for selection in education is extremely strong; it is a powerful feature of the Tory Mind. I have shown its association with a number of other ideological beliefs or assumptions: the first is that different kinds of children *need* different kinds of school and curricula; the second is that selection according to ability is more efficient (and that only a few exceptional teachers can cope with mixed-ability groups); a third belief is connected with cost — that a selective system is cheaper because the less academic children do not need some of the expensive courses and equipment that are necessary for more able children; a fourth assumption is that there is a relation between academic ability and social class (and therefore 'our' children deserve something better than what is provided for the majority). Underlying all those assumptions is the existing class structure. It is not unreasonable to perceive selection as part of the process of preserving that aspect of the status quo.

Selection: Some Problems

First, the idea that different kinds of children need different educational treatment is true in the sense that every child is a unique individual with interests and abilities not exactly the same as those of any other child. Schools and teachers have a responsibility to cater for such individuality, but that is not to say that children of any age can be conveniently grouped into categories such as academic/non academic, or high/low IQ. Nor does it mean that children can be fairly and appropriately selected at 11 for a grammar school, a technical school or a secondary modern school curriculum. Evidence on the 11+ testing in the 1960s showed that there was always a high percentage of mistakes or wrong predictions (Vernon, 1969). The nature of human differences is far more complex than any system of categories yet invented. And the latest studies of intelligence, for example, would suggest that there are at least seven kinds of intelligence rather than a single ability measured by one test (Gardner, 1983). Before the issue of selection became so highly politicized, opinion was moving in the direction of suggesting that whilst selection of some kind in education was eventually inevitable, it should be delayed as long as possible — age 11 was much too young for a final decision — and where possible selection should be self-selection, as it is in some other countries.

Second, the idea that selection is more efficient cannot be maintained. There was a long dispute about the examination results of comprehensive schools compared with those of selective schools which was inconclusive even in terms of crude performance scores, and those who advocated selection and segregation took no account of the unfairness and the mistakes involved.

Third, it may be true that a selective system would be cheaper if less money were allocated to the supposedly less academic children, but this raises additional problems of equity and efficiency: in a democracy is it *fair* to give less education to those who need it most? In an advanced industrial and commercial society, is it efficient to be satisfied that a majority could be grossly undereducated?

The fourth assumption relates ability to class. There is a statistical correlation but the evidence is open to interpretation: there are problems about whether ability is the result of 'nature or nurture', the fairness of the tests and the class-based nature of schooling itself have been raised as issues. The whole question of class and educational opportunity is complex and cannot simply be sidelined, or solved by selection and segregation.

Selection: Contradictions

The situation has been further confused by John Major and other Conservatives talking of a 'classless society'. This is either dishonest or a move towards the kind of utopian thinking that Conservatives claim to despise. A capitalist society has to rest upon a class system of some kind. Given that John Major is not trying to deceive us, what does he mean by a classless society?

In the context of his speeches, one possible interpretation of 'classless society' is that what he wants is a society that is genuinely 'open to talent'. What he and others, including Margaret Thatcher, objected to in English society (and in the Tory Party) were the feudal vestiges which distort the class system: the old school tie, the old boy network, the privileges retained by the aristocracy and the gentry — the traditional upper classes. Margaret Thatcher in her memoirs was quite contemptuous of the old paternalist Tories such as Sir Ian Gilmour. Her comments about the time when she asked Lord Soames to resign are relevant: 'Christopher Soames was equally angry — but in a grander way. I got the distinct impression that he felt the natural order of things was being violated and that he was, in effect, being dismissed by his housemaid' (p. 151). (This is the nearest thing to a joke in the whole 900 pages.) What we have here is the new Conservative group wishing to demonstrate that they no longer accept that they should be deferential to those who owe their position to birth and privilege. They are advocating a more thorough-going social mobility, but not that everyone is equal. A real classless society would be an egalitarian society, but Conservative policies on taxation are in themselves sufficient evidence to show that John Major does not intend that.

There is a dilemma for new Conservatives like John Major, John Patten, Norman Tebbitt and many others. Conservative ideology demands that change must be resisted until it is inevitable, yet to achieve a more socially mobile society, a number of radical changes would be essential, not least abolishing inherited titles, elite public schools, 'gentlemen's' clubs — to name but a few select and selective institutions. In fact to achieve complete social mobility it would be necessary to eliminate inherited wealth and the advantages of more caring and knowledgeable parents. A classless society would have to involve much more state control over all kinds of resources — including knowledge. A strange destination for a Tory Party to aspire to.

So what does John Major want? Not a classless society, not a society with 'perfect' social mobility, but a society where he feels socially more at ease — namely one in which he would not feel inferior to those who benefited from their 'breeding', elite schooling and other privileges that the upper classes take for granted as something they are entitled to. But if John Major ever really tried to implement even a mild version of such policies, he would split the Party into the traditional Tories and the radical modernizers. Or perhaps a 'classless society' is just rhetoric to retain the support of those who want to 'get on' without thinking through what achieving such a society would have to involve. In any case, it amounts to a serious ideological contradiction.

Key word 2: Traditional Curriculum and Teaching Methods

All sensible members of society have a respect for cultural traditions. In addition, teachers have a professional duty to preserve the best of our cultural heritage and transmit it to the next generation. But there comes a point when too much concern for tradition may impede ways of dealing with the present and the future. It is a question of balance. Some Tories, it would seem, want to sacrifice the present and the future on the altar of past traditions.

Traditional Methods: Some Problems

The National Curriculum was, for example, a political rather than an educational programme. Most teachers have accepted the National Curriculum in principle but regard the 1988 version of it as backward looking — little different from the Secondary Regulations of 1904. An opportunity for modernization was missed. Those planning a curriculum (and it is worth noting that the curriculum is a problem that cannot be solved by market forces) need to be sensitive *both* to traditions (cultural heritage) and the need to keep up to date. It is not an easy balance to achieve but it is essential. The easy solution is always to look back and to copy. Such a solution was easy but quite inadequate as a prescription for the 1990s and the twenty-first century.

Similarly, Conservatives tend to make a general assumption that traditional methods are better than modern or 'progressive' practices. It is true that education, like any other changing field, is subject to fads and fashions, but there is no evidence that teachers have been captured by them. Most teachers either stick mainly to traditional methods or are eclectic in employing a judicious mixture of traditional and new methods. Research has shown that there are very few completely 'progressive' teachers in our primary schools and even fewer in secondary schools (Bennett, 1976).

Conservatives, on the other hand, tend automatically to prefer the traditional: knowing how to use calculators is inferior to learning tables by heart and knowing how to do long division; correct spelling and grammar are more important than developing fluency and appropriate styles; learning dates in history is more important than understanding the nature of evidence. Tories have a general tendency to try to solve today's problems (and tomorrow's) by reverting to yesterday's methods.

This aspect of the Tory Mind can be seen throughout the years 1979–94 in relation to teacher education. An analysis of anti-teacher education texts (for example, Anthony O'Hear, 1988) reveals the following. First, a suspicion of all theory, which in the case of teacher education is extended to questioning the nature of 'education theory' and dismissing it on the grounds that it is not real theory like scientific theory. No mention is made of those philosophers who have shown that education theory is different in kind from scientific theory and should be judged by different criteria. Second, the Right alleges that much of education theory is particularly suspect because it is, allegedly, left-wing. It includes the kind of sociology which focuses on inequalities — of class, race and gender — which Tories find unnecessary. It also includes the kind of psychology which produces evidence to criticize intelligence tests, selection and streaming. And, perhaps worse still, education theory includes the kind of philosophy which encourages teachers (and pupils) to ask 'why?' rather than accept authority in an unquestioning way. To many Tories education theory is subversive. The Tory view is that teachers should be trained first by acquiring adequate knowledge and secondly by being shown how to communicate their knowledge with enthusiasm. For this kind of apprenticeship model, learning by doing in the classroom is to be preferred to discussing theory in a university. Unfortunately for the children, this is a completely static model of teacher training and of education, even if it were a practical possibility, which is very doubtful.

Traditional Methods: Some Contradictions
Unlike Tory politicians, most teachers understand the importance of balance — a respect for cultural heritage and well-established methods *together with* new improved techniques supported, if possible, by research. The teaching of reading is a good example. Tories demand better standards of reading but are obsessed with traditional methods. If teachers took their advice and tried to teach by the alphabet and phonics alone, standards of reading really would decline. Similarly,

Conservatives want young people to be well prepared for modern technology but often object to the use of word processors in the classroom.

Key word 3: Experts and Theories

To some extent this key word is related to 'traditional methods' above. Theory is open to suspicion partly because it tends to question some traditions in schools and suggest improved methods. This is not, of course, the whole explanation — a long-standing feature of the Tory Mind is to be suspicious of all theories and experts. Tories, in addition to assuming that traditional methods are best, are also critical of experts and theories in education for two other reasons. The first is that intellectuals and experts are automatically suspect because they are assumed to be against pragmatism and 'common sense'. The second, more extreme view, is that intellectuals and experts in education (the much condemned 'educational establishment') are frequently dismissed as left-wing conspirators.

Experts and Theories: Some Problems

Paul Black has provided an excellent example of this kind of ideologically-based anti-intellectualism:

> I start with a quotation from Kenneth Clarke from the Westminster Lecture (June 1991) when he was Secretary of State.
> 'The British pedagogues' hostility to written examinations of any kind can be taken to ludicrous extremes. The British left believe that pencil and paper examinations impose stress on pupils and demotivate them. We have tolerated for twenty years an arrangement whereby there is no national testing or examination of any kind for most pupils until they face GCSE at the age of 16 . . . This remarkable national obsession lies behind the more vehement opposition to the recent introduction of seven year old testing. They were made a little too complicated and we have said we will simplify them . . . The complications themselves were largely designed in the first place in an attempt to pacify opponents who feared above all else paper and pencil tests . . . This opposition to testing and examinations is largely based on a folk memory in the left about the old debate on the 11+ and grammar schools.' (Black in Chitty and Simon, 1993, p. 51 and p. 53)

Black explained some technical points about assessment and testing, and then went on to say:

> All of this reasoning was in the TGAT Report. It is deeply disturbing to have it rejected because it was 'complicated' and because it was 'designed to pacify opponents'. I do not mind if our arguments are confronted with counter-argument and evidence, but I find it offensive to have them attacked by imputation of the motives of the group which I chaired . . . The second feature of the arguments in the passage is even more disturbing. Opposition and opposing arguments are lumped together. If one asks, 'Who is being attacked here?', then it appears that in the first line it is 'The British pedagogue'; on the next line this becomes 'The British left'. Near the end, there is a clear reference to the TGAT Group. The reasons given by some groups, which were not TGAT's reasons, are lumped together in a single linked wave of criticism. This stereotyping of all expert opinion and evidence is very common in political argument. The effect that I have noticed is that many of us who really believe in the value of tough and reliable assessments are being bracketed together with those opposed to all testing, and are thereby labelled as woolly-minded. (in Chitty and Simon, 1993, pp. 51–3)

Experts and Theories: Some Contradictions

The result of such negative attitudes is that Tories tend to dismiss research findings along with modern methods with the result that some traditional practices and procedures are clung to long after they have ceased to be useful. The 'A' Level is an obvious example of this. Conservatives want to expand education and training for the 16–19 age group but at the same time are committed to a system in which 'A' Level is regarded as the gold standard and everything else is second best. But it is clearly the case that 'A' Level studies do not suit more than a small minority of the age group — and even for them the curriculum provided is much too narrow for the 1990s. The Higginson Report's carefully-argued reforms were dismissed on the grounds that they would lower standards; in practice, retaining the 'A' Level system prevents more students reaching higher standards.

Key word 4: Choice and the Market

Since 1979 (and indeed for some years before) 'choice' has been an important plank in Tory education policies. This is partly a move to legitimize private schools (in the cause of the 'right to choose'), but it is more than that: parental choice is the slogan which gives the individualism of the market priority over social planning.

Choice and the Market: Some Problems
This is an example of the Tory tendency to pay regard to ideological prejudices rather than evidence. There is now increasing evidence to show that the Tory preference for choice is fraught with difficulties. Probably the best summary of the situation is Michael Adler (1993) *An Alternative Approach to Parental Choice* (NCE Briefing 13). This shows quite clearly that parental choice has resulted in wasteful use of resources; on balance the gains from choice have been relatively small compared with the losses; and the result of aggregating individual choices, which may themselves be rational, is a situation which is irrational (an individual parent has to make a choice without knowing what choices other parents are making). The idea that competition makes teachers work harder to improve their school does not stand up to investigation.

Choice and the Market: Some Contradictions
If choice and the market are superior to planning, why have the Conservatives legislated for a compulsory National Curriculum? Why have compulsory schooling 5–16? The answer must be that for some purposes children need to be protected from the irresponsibility or lack of knowledge of their own parents. In some matters, and education is certainly one of them, choice and the market are not sufficient. Education is not a commodity to be bought and sold but a complex service for the whole community. The question of a market in education will be reviewed in more detail in chapter 8.

Key word 5: Expenditure

All Parties when in power are attracted by ideas which will reduce expenditure. Education, like health, could be a bottomless pit, and limits on spending have to be imposed. The Tories for fifteen years have placed a very high priority on making economies in education: the Thatcher memoirs show that she suspected that much educational expenditure was wasteful; Nigel Lawson was particularly critical of LEA high spending and unaccountability. The impression is that Conservatives were indulging in cost-cutting rather than cost-benefit analyses.

Expenditure: Some Problems

Unfortunately many of the bright ideas to cut costs have resulted in increased expenditure — for example, City Technology Colleges, student loans, school-based teacher training. And many real savings have been off-set by ideological innovations which have proved to be very expensive — for example, the Assisted Places Scheme, Grant Maintained Schools and National Curriculum assessment with the publication of league tables. National Curriculum assessment alone has cost £469m from 1988 to 1992 (with about £35m spent on the 1993 tests which hardly anyone used.)

Expenditure: Some Contradictions

Tories are also open to the charge of wanting to reduce the cost per pupil in state schools whilst sending their own children to private schools where the unit costs are considerably higher. One reasonable cost for the affluent but a much lower cost for the majority? Education is expensive and there comes a point where economies can only be made by reducing quality.

Key word 6: Centralization

Since 1979, and especially since 1988, there has been a relentless shift of power to the central authority in education. One excuse for this is a negative one: the hostility of the Conservative government towards all LEAs but particularly 'left-wing' authorities. In addition to those many examples of depriving LEAs of educational powers and responsibilities, there have been several other significant moves towards central control:

* national curriculum and assessment;
* universities;
* teacher education.

Even in those cases where services have been privatized there has been a move towards central control: school inspection has been privatized but the central OFSTED machinery has to supervise the inspection system from a central base closely linked to the DFE whereas in the past inspection was largely a local, LEA responsibility. The motives behind this kind of centralization are disturbingly anti-democratic. First, there is the mistrust motive: when the government knows best, everyone else has to be controlled — including local government. Second, it is not uncommon for governments in advanced capitalist societies, facing the increasing complexity of the state machinery and the difficulty of meeting expectations, to seek more and more control. This helps to explain why Thatcherism consisted of both more central control (strong government) and the promise of more individual freedom.

Centralization: Some Problems

Because there has been a long tradition of partnership, or at least of shared control in education, the central machinery is inadequate to exert direct supervision over thousands of schools in the system. Kenneth Baker, for example, thought that his reforms would necessitate a considerably enlarged inspectorate. But Margaret Thatcher turned down his suggestion of an additional 800 inspectors to supervise the National Curriculum. The 'solution' has been to centralize and then to create more quangos which are, of course, unaccountable locally and responsible only to the Education Secretary nationally.

Centralization: Some Contradictions

Increased central control is possibly the most serious and contradictory of all Tory innovations: many traditional checks and balances have been removed, leaving the Secretary of State with incredible powers. This is quite the opposite of declared policy intentions and it contradicts very fundamental Conservative beliefs in limited government and sharing the control of education with local authorities. I will return to this point in Part III.

Summary

From 1979–94 there has been an enormous amount of legislation on education. If those changes had been part of a process of building a magnificent modern system there would be few complaints. Unfortunately, the legislation has been a mixture of attempts to enforce ideological prejudices, out-of-date traditions and then more legislation to patch up earlier over-hasty drafting. Not all of it has been disastrous, but some opportunities to modernize have been missed: for example, the idea of a National Curriculum, which was welcomed in principle, was distorted by the ideology of choice and the market. The result is a system with demoralized teachers who have had to cope with too many changes in too short a time — a situation that could have been avoided by anyone with a little respect for research evidence. By 1994 there was no sign of a diminution of ideology under Major (see, in particular, the Jarvis–Major correspondence summarized in chapter 5). Education policy since 1991 has seemed to be lurching from one disaster to another.

Part III

The Future

So far I have been describing Tory policies and legislation since 1979 and have tried to explain the policies on education in the context of Tory dogmatics and ideology. In this final part I want to look to the future, so far as that is possible, in order to try to judge how adequately the Tory Mind could cope with education in the twenty-first century.

Chapter 7 will outline the requirements of a modern educational service, and will examine the match between those needs and the limitations imposed by Tory dogmatics.

Chapter 8 will revisit the Tory Mind and answer two crucial questions: is it possible to run a modern education system on a market principle? If not, can the Conservatives plan a modern education service suitable for the twenty-first century?

Chapter 7

The Needs of a Modern Education Service

Reliance on books, pens and paper could decrease as a consequence of developments in lap-top computing, communications technology and large-scale, remotely accessible, multi-media data bases . . . Obstacles to any such developments in education will not come from scientific or technological constraints. Rather, they will arise from political, economic and ideological considerations. (D. Wood, 1993, p. 1)

People say there is too much jargon, so let me give you some of my own: knowledge, discipline, tables, dates, Shakespeare, *British* history, standards, English grammar, spelling, marks, tests and good manners. (John Major to the Conservative Women's Conference, June 1993)

I have elsewhere (Lawton, 1992) outlined what I believed, a few years ago, to be the priorities for developing a modern education service. It would be less valuable to repeat that exercise here than to find another independent and more recent model. For that purpose I will make use of the report of the National Commission on Education *Learning to Succeed* (1993) which deliberately attempted to produce a plan completely without political bias. In so far as it is possible to be ideology-free, it is. The report sets out to prescribe an adequate and appropriate education service for a democratic society — the UK — with its unique history and traditions. The composition of the Commission was carefully non-Party and with a mixture of lay and professional members. (It is perhaps a sign of the times that, as a fully paid up member of the educational establishment, I have to declare myself to be 'biased'.)

The NCE Report

The NCE Report begins with a description of its 'vision' or 'mission statement', consisting of seven points which would, I think, be shared by the vast majority of the population of the UK, including most Conservative politicians. If I am right in that assumption, the report will provide a useful and fair basis, not only for judging Conservative progress to date, but also for evaluating their prospects for the future. It is a very important document and should be read in full by anyone concerned with education in the UK. The summary that follows in this chapter is *not* intended as a substitute for a complete reading.

The seven points of the vision are:

1   In all countries knowledge and applied intelligence have become central to economic success, and personal and social well-being.
2   In the United Kingdom much higher achievement in education and training is needed to match world standards.
3   Everyone must want to learn, and have ample opportunity and encouragement to do so.
4   All children must achieve a good grasp of literacy and basic skills early on as the foundation for learning throughout life.
5   The full range of people's abilities must be recognized and their development rewarded.
6   High quality learning depends above all on the knowledge, skill, effort and example of teachers and trainers.
7   It is the role of education *both* to interpret and pass on the values of society, *and* to stimulate people to think for themselves and to change the world around them.

The vision was supported by seven goals necessary for the achievement of the vision. But before proceeding to the goals, the Commission summarized the strengths and weaknesses of the present system:

It is possible to summarise the results at present achieved by education and training in the UK quite briefly. A minority of academically able young people receive a good, if narrow, education and, for them, provision is well suited and efficiently run. For a majority of young people, education is of more variable benefit. The talents of many are not valued enough and not developed enough; and once they start work, the same is true in terms of training. In addition, an uncomfortably large minority of young people leaving school have trouble with literacy and numeracy and seem to have benefited all too little from their education. (p. 1)

To check the fairness of that statement comparisons were made with achievements in other countries. At age 16 and 18 the standards in England are lower. I will not reproduce all the comparative data here, but one table will indicate the nature of the problem:

Table 2:   Young people obtaining a comparable upper secondary school qualification at 18+, 1990

Country	Percentages
Germany	68
France	48
Japan	80
England	29

(NCE, 1993, p. 3)

The figures for 16 year olds and those who leave school at 16 for employment are just as worrying in terms of qualifications (or lack of qualifications).

As well as the general low level of achievement, there is another point to which the NCE drew attention: the fact that at all levels — pre-school, school and HE — chances, or opportunities, are not the same for all individuals. Class is still a major determining factor. (Halsey (1992) in a separate Briefing Paper showed that the proportions of working-class boys and girls reaching university have hardly improved since 1944.)

The vision was supplemented by seven goals:

1   High quality nursery education must be available for all 3 and 4 year olds.
2   There must be courses and qualifications that bring out the best in every pupil.
3   Every pupil in every lesson has the right to good teaching and adequate support facilities.
4   Everyone must be entitled to learn throughout life and be encouraged in practice to do so.
5   The management of education and training must be integrated and those with a stake in them must have this recognized.
6   There must be greater public and private investment in education and training to achieve a better return.
7   Achievement must constantly rise and progress be open for all to examine.

The rest of the report examined how those goals could be achieved.

With the exception of goal 1, however, it would be possible to express agreement with all of the goals in general terms without commitment to specific action. I will, therefore, include for analysis the more detailed recommendations made by NCE. Where appropriate I will also include some useful details found not in the main text of the report but in the separate Briefing Papers.

1 The 3 to 4 Year Old Age Group

Throughout the United Kingdom there are wide variations in provision for children below compulsory school age ... This diversity does not mean effective choice for parents, still less the guarantee of high quality educational experience for young children. (p. 111)

* High-quality, publicly-funded, nursery education should be provided for all 3 to 4 year olds.
* The priority for implementation should be in deprived areas where the 100 per cent target should be met within five years.
* After that, the following targets should be met:
   within ten years 60 per cent of all 3 to 4 year olds in all areas;
   within fifteen years 95 per cent of all 4 year olds;
   within fifteen years 85 per cent of all 3 year olds.
* Funding should be made available from central government.
* A planned curriculum for 3 to 5 year olds should be provided.

The arguments in favour of this programme are powerful. There is a need and demand for this service; not only is England behind other European countries in this provision, but research evidence shows that even in purely economic terms, good quality education at the age of 3 to 5 years pays. American research, such as Schweinhart and Weikart (1993) shows a direct cost-benefit relationship between early education, and less delinquency and unemployment later.

2 Compulsory Schooling 5 to 16

Good schools are at the heart of good education. Raising educational achievement to much higher levels in the coming decades demands an all-round improvement in quality. (p. 141)

* Primary school pupil–teacher ratios (PTR) in England and Wales are among the least favourable in OECD countries and *are increasing*: primary class sizes should be reduced and a provisional target of 20 is suggested.
* The NCE found general support for the idea of a National Curriculum and no support for abandoning the principle of a National Curriculum, which has two facets — responsibility and entitlement. Specific recommendations included that the compulsory part of the National Curriculum should be slimmed down; life skills should be given greater importance and be broadened to include citizenship, and a modern foreign language. In order to avoid giving the impression that 16 is the *normal* school leaving age, the curriculum for the age group 14–18 should be planned as a whole (16–18 becoming Key Stage 5 — see below).
* Performance in literacy and numeracy should be raised
    by early intervention;
    by emphasis on basic skills in primary school;
    by incentives and support for improving literacy and numeracy skills throughout schooling;
    by Reading Recovery schemes;
    by parental participation;
    by well-defined standards.

(Other recommendations overlap with teacher education and will be considered under that heading.)

* Independent schools should be required to follow the National Curriculum.
* National Curriculum assessment: more attention should be paid to teacher assessment; teacher assessment and external test results should be provided separately.
* The publication of assessment results should be accompanied by warnings about data interpretation; and schools should be listed alphabetically not in league tables.
* Learning in schools should be improved by the encouragement of new techniques such as 'flexible learning'.
* Diversity should be encouraged within schools rather than between schools, thus eliminating the need for choice of schools.
* Increased selection by ability should be discouraged; schools should be able to teach effectively the full range of ability they admit.

* The aim should be for all schools to be effective schools offering choices; the Assisted Places Scheme should then be phased out in appropriate stages.
* All schools should be able to cope adequately with children with special needs.

The evidence for the need to improve PTR in primary schools is strong (Mortimore and Blatchford, 1993), and in England the difference between maintained and private schools is striking in this respect:

Table 3:   Average number of pupils per teacher (PTR) in England by phase (1991)

Phase	PTR
Primary	22.2
Secondary	15.5
Non-maintained (private)	10.8
All Schools	17.3

(from *NCE Briefing 12*, p. 3)

The general principle governing the detailed recommendations about compulsory schooling would seem to be that *all* schools should be effective schools and that this should be where policy priorities should be directed — not by attempting to raise standards by selecting some children and some schools for preferential treatment. Briefing Paper No. 7 (Walford, 1992) also argues strongly in favour of an alternative to selection.

The National Curriculum is an example of attempting to raise standards overall: this should become the way for all reforms.

3 Education and Training 16 to 19

Our system has concentrated for too long on the needs of the academically able at the expense of the rest. All young people reaching the age of 16, whatever their abilities, need to be able to see a clearly signposted way forward and to have an opportunity to build on what they have already achieved. All young people should feel that they will benefit if they go on to some form of structured post-compulsory educational training. There needs to be a framework for learning and a system of support which provides the necessary encouragement and the incentives to do so. (p. 239)

* Staying on full time after 16 should become the norm.
* Those who leave full-time education at 16 or 17 should be encouraged to work for a qualification.
* A new General Education Diploma (GED) should be introduced, replacing GCSE, 'A' Levels and vocational qualifications; the GED will be a grouped award. 'We wish to see academic and vocational routes intersecting, having equal esteem and receiving equal support.' (p. 252)
* By 1996 all employees should take part in training or development activities; by 1996, 50 per cent of the workforce should be aiming at four National Vocational Qualifications (NVQ)/Scottish Vocational Qualifications (SVQ) or units towards them; by 2000, 50 per cent of the workforce should be qualified to NVQ/SVQ or equivalent; by 1996, 50 per cent of medium to large organizations to be 'investors in people'; by 2000 at least 90 per cent should be working for qualifications until 18.
* There should be compulsory Further Education of one and a half days per week for all 16–17 year olds not in full-time education.
* New financial support arrangements should be introduced for the 16+ group.

4 Higher Education

In a society in which knowledge and applied intelligence are central, higher education is at the heart of the country's well-being. Universities have a mission to pursue and transfer new knowledge; to help to manage and apply the international knowledge explosion set off by modern communications and information technology; and to educate and train to the highest levels . . . (p. 289)

* More investment is needed in Higher Education.
* There should be a change of funding for students (not a graduate tax but a loan repayment scheme) for both full- and part-time students.
* More working-class students should be encouraged.

5 Lifelong Education

In recent years the idea that lifetime education and training is desirable has become accepted, but too often it attracts a dutiful genuflexion rather than enthusiasms. (p. 321)

The most dangerous people in Rover are those who have for-gotten how to change. If they are hit by change, they fear it and resist it. (p. 332)

* There should be an entitlement to continuing learning.
* There should be a coherent policy which builds upon employer training and encourages other agencies.
* Employers should be obliged to provide time off for educational training (a minimum of five days a year) and pay the fees.

6 Teacher Education and Training

Every pupil should be entitled in each lesson to be taught by a teacher with the knowledge, training, competence and commit-ment to teach that lesson well . . . (p. 193)

We are struck by the extent to which German and French education systems place responsibility on the shoulders of professional teachers. It contrasts sharply with the mood of distrust of the professionals which has grown in this country in recent years, not without government encouragement. (p. 340)

* There should better management in schools.
* A General Teaching Council for England and Wales should be established.
* All schools should have a policy for staff development; all teachers should have a personal development plan (used in teacher appraisal); every teacher should be entitled to two days each year for training outside the school.
* There should be induction programmes funded from central government; each new teacher should have a probationary period, normally of two years, with an entitlement to induction programmes and with a mentor allocated.

7 Management of Education and Training

The running of a national system of education and training is an extraordinarily demanding and complex task. (p. 339)

There have been attempts in the past to differentiate education sharply from training. In reality, there is no sharp division but rather a continuum . . . (p. 345)

* A Department for Education and Training (DET) should be created by merging DFE with those parts of the Employment Department responsible for training.
* The Office for Standards in Education would assume responsibility for inspecting training and its title would be amended to the Office for Standards in Education and Training (OFSET).
* There should be an intermediate tier of locally accountable bodies between the DET and individual schools — Education and Training Boards (ETB). City Technology Colleges should be within the aegis of ETBs.
* Responsibility for school inspection should be shared by ETBs and OFSET.

8 Funding

Our vision for education and training in the UK is ambitious but it is the minimum necessary for any reasonable set of economic and social goals that the nation should set itself. (p. 367)

* Greater public and private investment in education and training is needed.
* There should be additional spending of £3.2 billion a year (with savings proposed this would mean additional expenditure of about £1.4 billion).

I would like to stress that this report is not a madly ambitious plan for the future: indeed, the NCE has been criticized by some for being too cautious. But the report will serve as a set of modest and realistic 'benchmarks' (a favourite Conservative word in the 1980s) against which predictions of Conservative behaviour may be measured.

Comparison of Needs and Conservative Policies

How does the first part of this chapter compare with the Tory policies and achievements outlined in chapter 6?

1 3 to 4 Year Old Age Group

This is a phase which has received mixed messages from Tory politicians. In the 1972 White Paper, Margaret Thatcher herself accorded pre-school education a degree of priority, but the recommendation was never acted upon. Since 1979, pre-school education has not featured in any Election Manifesto and, in recent years, the Secretary of State has said that there is insufficient money available for expansion of pre-school provision (of the kind envisaged by NCE).

There is probably no ideological obstacle to meeting the NCE objective, although some Tories have occasionally expressed the view that children below the age of 5 are best cared for at home by their mothers. Money is a problem. The NCE plan has been estimated to cost about £800m. John Major seems to be convinced by the pragmatic advantages of better provision, but he has not yet committed himself to a specific action plan and, in January 1994, Robin Squire (Parliamentary Under-Secretary for Education), in answer to a Parliamentary Question, said that there was no money available. It may be unkind to point out that large sums of money have been found, however, for other projects such as the Assisted Places Scheme and City Technology Colleges. It all depends upon what the politicians' priorities are.

2 Compulsory Schooling 5 to 16

There are at least five separate issues here:

(i)   the size of primary classes — the quality of provision 5–11;
(ii) the National Curriculum and its assessment;
(iii) teaching methods;
(iv) diversity/selection;
(v)   children with special educational needs.

I will consider each separately.

(i) Class Size/Quality
Superficially the problem here would seem to be one of cost. Smaller classes are obviously expensive and the present trend towards larger classes is not accidental, but a deliberate attempt to bring down unit costs in primary schools. Tories have frequently resorted to the argument that there is no proof that smaller classes increase quality. Peter Mortimore and Peter Blatchford were asked by NCE to look at the

evidence on this question. They wrote *The Issue of Class Size* (1993) as NCE Briefing No. 12. They concluded that although research evidence was not entirely clear-cut 'from recent work in the US, it appears that pupils educated in smaller classes during the first four years of schooling, out-perform pupils in larger classes and maintain their academic advantage and demonstrate increased participation two years later. Children from disadvantaged backgrounds benefit most from smaller classes' (p. 1).

The Tory attitude is more than a little hypocritical: when parents make a choice between private schools and maintained schools, one important factor is class size. Parents are often prepared to pay for this aspect of private education, yet it seems that this 'choice' is only available to those who can afford to pay. There may be no automatic improvement in reducing class size, but class size is a feature of schools that parents would choose if they could. Thus the question of cost is mixed up with ideology: Tory privatizers and minimalists believe that parents should have the right to pay for something better than state provision. If all differences in class size were removed, then this kind of choice would no longer be available; some Tories are torn between wanting to achieve better quality for all whilst seeking to retain a privileged position for their own children. This is particularly the case with class size, but it applies to questions of quality more generally. There is a danger of raising quality so high that private education becomes either even more expensive or less of a privilege — what is the point of choice if choosing does not mean 'better'? We are a long way away from that position but it would seem to be an aspect of the thinking of some Tories. This would be the inverse of that 'envy' with which Conservatives sometimes change socialists. In any case, it is very unlikely that a Conservative government will embark on a policy of improving the pupil–teacher ratio at a time when the major target is to reduce public expenditure.

(ii) National Curriculum Assessment

On this issue we move very definitely into an ideological area. The Dearing Final Report (1994), which was immediately accepted by the Conservative government has pruned the National Curriculum down to a core curriculum (especially for the 14–16 age group), but failed to grasp the real nettle of assessment. All the problems of National Curriculum assessment in 1993 stemmed from the Tory failure to accept the TGAT recommendations about teacher assessment. Ideologically, Tories find it difficult to trust the teachers (in state schools). But for National Curriculum assessment to work effectively, teachers must be trusted (as well as given additional training). This Conservative failure not only involves National Curriculum assessment, but other aspects of quality in the teaching–learning situation. Unless teachers are treated as professionals (as teachers in good private schools expect to be) they will not produce the kind of changes in quality referred to in the first section of this chapter — for example, Reading Recovery and other schemes involving parental participation.

The Tory Mind seems to regard teachers as semi-skilled workers (see Linda Darling-Hammond *et al.*, 1983) who need to be told exactly what to do and supervised to ensure that they carry out instructions. This attitude is a major impediment to raising standards and improving quality in primary and secondary schools.

(iii) Teaching Methods

The NCE suggest that schools should be encouraged to develop innovative teaching methods. This is also doubly difficult in terms of the Tory Mind. First, Tories appear to be obsessed with traditional methods; teachers are frequently criticized for developing 'trendy' new techniques — Tories do not trust teachers' expertise and judgment; in addition, Tories do not want teachers to be accorded that kind of professional status in any case.

(iv) Diversity/Selection

The Tory mind tends to give high priority to differentiation between pupils in terms of ability and to see selection as the organizational means of achieving it. It is ideologically very difficult to make that attitude compatible with the NCE principle of encouraging diversity *within* schools and discouraging selection by ability. As we have seen, one of the consistent trends since 1979 has been the reintroduction of selection in various forms — for example, the Assisted Places Scheme, City Technology Colleges and some Grant Maintained schools being permitted to introduce selection. The difficulty here is ideological rather than financial. The Tory Mind is strongly attached to selection in principle and practice, and has, since 1979, paid high prices for the three schemes mentioned above to achieve selection.

(v) Special Educational Needs

The NCE recommended that all schools should be able to cope with children with special educational needs. To some extent this issue is related — practically and ideologically — to the question of selection (and segregation). In practice, some of the 'choice and market' policies being pursued actually discourage schools from accepting pupils with special needs and, of course, catering adequately for such children is extremely expensive. There is evidence that some schools have taken the easy way out by leaving the ESN problem to other schools. The Warnock policy of 'integration' may, ironically and unintentionally, result in a drift of children with special educational needs to 'sink' schools.

3 Education and Training 16–19

The Tory Mind tends to make a sharp ideological distinction between education and tráining which would impede many of the NCE proposals. Training itself is accorded low status, being associated with low-level manual work rather than the kind of training received by doctors and lawyers. In the 1990s, training may be even more deserving of attention than education. It is also important to clarify the distinction between education and training. There are important differences between them, but the Tory desire to keep them segregated organizationally is potentially disastrous. Many others have agreed with the NCE Report on this question. In 1990, John Cassells produced *Britain's Real Skill Shortage* for the Policy Studies Institute recommending a new qualification at 18+ covering academic and vocational, full-time and part-time courses. In the same year, Christopher Ball wrote *More Means Different* for the RSA emphasizing the need to widen access to universities and questioning the future of 'A' Levels. In 1991, the Secondary Heads Association, the Committee of Vice-Chancellors and Principals, and the Association of Principals of Sixth Form Colleges (APVIC), as well as the Royal Society, all declared in favour of the reform of 'A' Level and a unified national post-16 framework.

4 Higher Education

The Conservatives have gone some way towards the expansion of HE: partly by abolishing the binary line between polytechnics and universities (and at a stroke increasing the total number of university places available); partly by encouraging the expansion of numbers within institutions. They have reached their own self-imposed target of one in three young people going on to higher education, but they show no sign of interest in the three other proposals of the NCE: more investment in the institutions; a better system of funding the students; and, most important of all, encouraging more working-class students. Whilst they seem reluctant to tackle all three proposals, the last is the most difficult one for them ideologically: they are opposed to spending money on this problem and, in addition, they are always anxious lest it be a 'levelling down' and are inclined to believe that it always is. This explains government reactions to improved results in the GCSE and the 'more means worse' slogan of the 1970s. (It is also interesting that we compare very unfavourably with such countries as Germany in terms of the numbers of working-class students in higher education.) Recent policies have been criticized by Vice-Chancellors and others for making it more difficult (or at least less attractive) for working-class students to reach university and complete their courses.

5 Lifelong Education

The Tory Mind has shown little interest in this concept. There is no mention of it in recent policy documents, although other reviews of the education system, such as that of Sir Christopher Ball (1990 and 1991), have made 'the learning society' a central feature of education policy.

6 Teacher Education and Training

The Tory Mind, as we have seen, distrusts many kinds of professional expertise, prefers learning by experience to theory, and is particularly suspicious of education theory and its use as part of the education and training of teachers. The 1993 Bill is moving precisely in the opposite direction to NCE proposals by separating teacher training from the rest of higher education and for making teacher training more like a school-based apprenticeship.

7 Management of Education and Training

Two of the NCE main proposals are directly in conflict with current Tory thinking: having a single department for Education and Training, and strengthening *local* responsibility for both education and training. The Tory Mind seems to be determined to keep education and training separate for ideological reasons; and the resignation in 1993 of Sir Geoffrey Holland, Permanent Secretary at the DFE, was said to be connected with his failure to convince the Education Secretary and the Prime Minister of the need to bring education and training together in a single Ministry.

Introducing Education and Training Boards (ETBs) at local level would also be running counter to all the current trends in controlling finance and policy from the centre — although the more traditional Tory view was in favour of strong local government. Major and Patten have shown no inclination to move back to a partnership model.

8 Funding

The increased spending recommended by the NCE (£1.4 billion) would not be impossible for a government committed to education reform, but the Conservative priority in 1993–94 was still undoubtedly the reduction of public spending and the PSBR. It is extremely unlikely that any Tory Chancellor of the Exchequer could be persuaded to change that policy for the sake of improving state education — nor would there be much backbench support for such a move.

Conclusion

The match between the educational needs of a modern society and Tory policy priorities is clearly not close after fifteen years of uninterrupted rule. This is partly, but not entirely, because they have invested so much in choice and the market.

The final chapter will examine the whole question of market choice policies in education as well as the alternative possibility to Tory educational planning for the twenty-first century.

Chapter 8

The Tory Mind Revisited: Markets or Planning?

Hayek's development of the concept of a spontaneous natural order provided a strong philosophical underpinning for the market, not least by demonstrating that our understanding of the nature of society and the economy is too partial to admit economic management by the state. Economic planning was both impossible and unnecessary. (Nigel Lawson, 1992, p. 14)

We must refresh our understanding of the moral case against the welfare state. Much of what we call the welfare state should be returned to civil society, especially education and health care . . . (David G. Green, 1993, p. 152)

By the time of the next General Election the possible life-span of the next government will take us into the twenty-first century. How convinced should we be that the Conservatives, even if they embark upon a series of tactical U-turns on education policy, can cope with the educational needs of a modern industrial democratic society?

There will be three sections in this chapter: the first part will recapitulate and develop some ideas about the Tory Mind, concentrating on the 1994 vintage beliefs, values and attitudes; the second will closely examine the Conservative Party claims for providing education by means of choice and markets; and the third will look at the possibility of a Tory plan for education and the likelihood of it being satisfactory, bearing in mind the evidence of chapters 6 and 7.

The Tory Mind Revisited

In earlier chapters I have sketched the features of the Tory Mind, mainly from the evidence of speeches and publications as well as legislation. The most important feature of the Tory Mind is the need to find inspiration in the past rather than in the future, although Tory and neo-liberal wings look to different (real or supposed) aspects of the past. In education this becomes an exaggerated concern for tradition and old-fashioned teaching methods. Our examination of legislation 1979–94 (in chapter 6) showed five other significant characteristics: a concern to *select* pupils; a dislike of *experts and theory*; a desire to reduce *ex-penditure*; and a connected desire to *centralize control* in order to diminish the power of local authorities; and last but by no means least, an increasing concern to support parental *choice* as a means of intro-ducing *the market* into education. They are all 'backward-looking' except the increased central control which is a deviation from a pure Tory point of view. It, by contrast to the others, is often justified by reference to the similar centralization of education in major competitor countries — with a tendency to ignore current decentralizing initiatives in some of those countries.

Since 1979 perhaps the most significant development has been what might be called the Hayek-Lawson line that economic planning is impossible and that bureaucracies are inferior to market forces in man-aging future needs: prediction is impossible, so all planning is a waste of resources. This dubious assumption, accompanied by an irrational faith in the market, has encouraged privatization in many fields, includ-ing some where state monopolies had hitherto been considered by almost everyone preferable to private enterprise and profit (for exam-ple, gas, electricity and water). Market forces have been introduced even more controversially into the national health service and educa-tion. It remains to be seen what the long-term outcomes will be in the case of gas and other services, but some of the disadvantages of market competition in the NHS are already clear — for example, surgeons with plenty of space on their lists being told not to deal with routine cases until the next financial year. In education I shall argue that market com-petition is not only inferior to forward planning, but also that some kinds of competition are harmful and ultimately destructive. The Conservative arguments in favour of choice and the market are over-simplified, divisive and sometimes dishonest.

Choice and the market have been the dominant features of Tory policy in the 1990s (and I shall return to that theme in the second part of this chapter), but some Conservatives have expressed concern at this. Scruton (1982), for example, has criticized the Party for embracing non-Conservative market ideas which have contaminated Conservative dogmatics by liberalism:

> The Party's links with conservativism are, however, uncertain, and it has recently exhibited a sympathy for liberal, and in

> particular, laissez-faire, doctrines in both politics and economics,
> and so distanced itself from its 19th century origins. (pp. 91–92)

I will refer to two more Conservative philosophers whose views have been influential in terms of the Tory Mind and Conservative policies — Quinton, whose earlier book was mentioned in chapter 1, and O'Hear. They present an alternative — traditional — basis for policies which might even replace the market as the dominant force in Conservative thinking.

Anthony Quinton, a very loyal supporter of the Conservative government in the House of Lords, has written about a traditional Tory concern which bears directly upon education. In the 1992 Victor Cook Memorial Lectures, Quinton chose as his theme, 'Culture, Education and Values'. Seeing education as part of a crisis in contemporary culture, Quinton complains that some teachers, reacting against the restrictions of a fixed literary canon, have rejected traditional views of literature altogether; others correctly seeing language as subject to change have gone to the illogical extreme of abandoning all notions of correctness in spelling and grammar, perhaps for the additional reason that it would be to impose middle-class standards on the working classes. Worse still is the attack on rationality itself at the hands of Foucault, Derrida and others. Quinton accepts that simply to know many facts is not to be educated, but believes that rejection of knowledge in favour of cognitive skills has gone too far. He also wants to retain the notion of high culture which he believes to be in danger.

In a very brief and partial history of education, Quinton shows the idea of a canon can be traced back to archaic Greece where formal education originally consisted of studying Homer, but was gradually extended to other texts. The canon in Greece and later in the rest of Europe was not merely an expression of respect for old texts, but a respect for the traditional values reflected in the texts, which today include nineteenth century novels and poetry.

He sees the attack on the idea of the canon as political — an objection to minority tastes being imposed upon the majority. (He quotes as evidence the scene of Jesse Jackson in the USA, leading 500 students at Stanford University chanting 'Ho, ho, ho, Western culture's got to go'.) He uses this example to attack not only those who would wish to rethink the canon but those who would reject evaluative literary criticism in favour of a new discipline, 'cultural studies'.

Quinton proceeds to an attack on fashionable thinkers like Derrida, presumably because he features in some cultural studies programmes. At this stage it becomes clear that for Quinton the main enemies are the 'undiscriminating relativists' who also attack science and its rationality, objectivity and disinterestedness. The lecture ends by slipping from that easy target to a condemnation of those teachers of English who see language rules as elitist.

Quinton begins his second lecture by assuming that he has demonstrated that the canon, intellectual values and linguistic skills are all repudiated by a 'militant egalitarianism'. But the only evidence cited is from the USA — he produces no evidence from the UK. He assumes that there is a 'political' attack on high culture and returns to his preference for the canon.

I have spent some time on those two lectures because Quinton's diagnosis is essentially a Conservative one. He looks back to the golden age of the canon, when the young were taught to write correct English and when traditional standards of scholarship were taken for granted. He does not like some of the current developments in schools and universities which he sees as a culture crisis, and is fearful about what the future might have in store. His solution to the crisis is to look back to a 'better yesterday' and to want to return to it, rather than trying to diagnose a changing situation in order to develop new methods of teaching and learning. Perhaps surprisingly, he shares the Tory politicians' belief in a left-wing egalitarian, anti-education plot.

A variant of this Conservative attitude is provided by Quinton's fellow Cook lecturer, Professor Anthony O'Hear (whose views on teacher education I mentioned in chapter 6). The first of his two titles is 'Education, Value and Awe' and he asks what is necessary to encourage a sense of awe in children in a context hostile to it. He contrasts two views of education: the first is education as a transmitter of culture and inculcator of values; the second is education as a process in which individuals are encouraged to question received opinion and values 'and to take it on themselves to decide what they will regard as valuable or not'. He puts the blame for the second view partly on the rationalism of the Enlightenment: Diderot is attacked for saying that a true philosopher would 'trample under foot prejudice, tradition, venerability, universal assent, authority — in a word, everything that overawes the crowd'; an individual should dare 'to think for himself' and 'to admit nothing save the testimony of his own reason and experience'. O'Hear makes clear his preference for an education which encourages the acceptance of traditional values and culture.

J. S. Mill is also criticized for his excessively rational approach which ends in prizing liberty above all else. Instead, according to O'Hear, we should have regard for Nietzsche and the subtle interrelationships that exist between value, culture, reason and education. He suggests that much of today's 'personal and social education', in the tradition of Schools Council Projects in Humanities and Moral Education, is guilty of that kind of over-rational relativism.

The contrasting (Aristotelian) expectation is that young people must first be encouraged to do what is good and virtuous; they will then feel attracted to it and be in a better position to reason about moral values. So far I suspect that many teachers would agree with O'Hear, but they might have doubts about his next step:

> Educators ought then to be more concerned with inculcating in the young a sense of awe and respect for the virtues of civilised life than with encouraging their pupils to regard these virtues as open to choice or simply a reification of defeasible preferences. A rationalistic approach to values and to education is likely to foster the latter attitude, whereas an education stressing custom and respect is likely to encourage the former. (O'Hear in Haldane, 1992, p. 53)

Teachers might want to know exactly what O'Hear meant by 'more concerned' or ask 'how much more?' O'Hear's method would be to use literature and the arts (not philosophy or the social sciences) — a carefully chosen canon.

In his second lecture O'Hear discusses education as a process of initiation into worthwhile forms of knowledge and experience — the pursuit of the excellent. Because, for reasons set out by Oakeshott (1989), such education is difficult and not attainable by all, selection is essential and examinations for all, like GCSE, are impossible. Similarly, 'A' Levels must be preserved because they meet the difficulty requirements suggested by Oakeshott. There is a curious reversal of comprehensive policies here: instead of attempting to make high culture accessible to all, there seems to be a suggestion that difficulty is valued for its own sake — or possibly as a means of selection.

O'Hear presents us with another interesting example of the Tory Mind (and one which has certainly been influential in terms of policy making). The basic principle, with which most teachers would surely agree, is that children should be encouraged to respect traditions and traditional values. In this sense all teachers are conservative. It is the leap from that position to automatic and unquestioning respect that will generate argument within the teaching profession. Good teachers develop the art of initiating children into the *living* traditions of literature, for example, which involves both the use of suitable contemporary works and getting children to become involved in the tradition — creative writing. O'Hear takes a curiously passive view of learning. But real care involves a more active engagement. The canon is the beginning of the learning process, not the end of it. Both Quinton and O'Hear seem to see the canon as something to be imposed on the learners, not as part of a living tradition.

The curriculum associated with O'Hear's pursuit of the excellent is also backward-looking: it is the grammar school curriculum of traditional subjects. A single examination for all is condemned, but no account is taken of arguments in favour of the GCSE (which was by no means a sudden decision, and was argued over for more than twenty years). Similarly, 'A' Levels must stay because they too represent traditional standards of excellence. No reference is made to the fact that secondary education for all has made new demands on schools and teachers. O'Hear also ignores other social and economic changes which make it necessary to rethink some aspects of schooling. This is not to deny the force of his arguments against relativism and in favour of traditions. The point I am making is that an important feature of the Tory Mind on education is that it exaggerates the importance of tradition, to the neglect of an engagement with current problems. To accept selection, the grammar school curriculum and 'A' Levels uncritically will undoubtedly limit the policy-making procedures and cause confusion and conflict. It is easy to accept O'Hear's idea of delaying criticism until understanding has been achieved (Richard Peters made a similar point about moral education many years ago), but this should not be used as a blanket prohibition of modern approaches to learning or of 'critical thinking'.

The views of Quinton and O'Hear (in Haldane, 1992) are important because they provide some intellectual underpinning to the traditional Tory Mind and its ideologies. A populist version of the same attitude may be seen in John Major's 'back to basics' speech in April 1993 to the Conservative Europe Group — 'a country of long shadows on county grounds, warm beer, invincible green suburbs, dog-lovers . . . and old maids bicycling to holy communion through the morning mist'. Conservatives naturally look back rather than to the future. Many possess an exaggerated value for the past — almost amounting to a romantic myth of a society in which workers knew their place, the Empire was proof of British superiority, differences in rank were taken for granted, and education helped to preserve stability and order. But perhaps even more important for education, Conservatives have a fear of the future: a fear of loss of order and stability, fear of a world in which property may be threatened by taxation and where privileges, including cultural privileges, may be swept away in the name of democracy. They believe that education should have been a means of guarding against this nightmare, but they fear that the service has been taken over by left-wing subversives. At times of cultural or economic crisis, fear and reactionary diagnoses become even more pronounced — sometimes hysterical. Many Conservative attitudes to schooling appear to be connected not only with a fear of the future, but with the conviction that there has been a deliberate plot to misuse education.

Choice and the Market

One of the surprising features of the period 1979–94 was the capture of the Conservative Party by advocates of market philosophies and parental choice. The Tory Mind has been corrupted by neo-liberal fantasies. This trend, as we saw in chapter 4, goes back further than 1979 — at least to the 1960s — but it was then a minority view; since 1979 it has not only gathered momentum but has also dominated two massive pieces of legislation — the 1988 and 1993 Education Acts. The arguments behind this ideology are superficially very simple: first, that bureaucracies are inefficient at organizing anything — including education — and that power should be devolved to the consumer (the parents); second, that competition is a better motivating force than cooperation; third, that parents give more support to schools that they choose; and, fourth, that pupils achieve better in schools which offer a degree of specialization. These are similar to the arguments advanced by Chubb and Moe (1990) in the USA, who also attack the notion of the control of education by 'local democracies' (see also the discussion of Ranson, 1993b, below).

Some of the evidence on the practical disadvantages of choice was given in chapter 6. Here I want to suggest not only that market choice has failed to improve educational standards but that the market is inappropriate for the education service in principle as well as in practice.

There are several different kinds of argument which lead to the same conclusion — that for a good education service the market is inferior to planning. The first argument involves a more general attack on the market. For example, Jonathan Rosenhead (1992), Professor of Operational Research at LSE, talks of 'the catastrophic retreat from reason in public affairs'. This kind of retreat from reason is focused on an irrational faith in the hidden hand which is somehow supposed to be superior to human reason:

> There is now a widespread, almost hegemonic ideology which
> incorporates a semi-mystical belief in the beneficial properties
> of market forces. The underlying assertions are
> (i) that through market forces individual preferences can find
> untrammelled expression;
> (ii) that the market handles the equilibration of supply and
> demand better than bureaucracy can; and,
> (iii) that free competition provides an automatic mechanism for
> achieving efficiency improvements.
> These assumptions underlie both the Conservative government
> programmes of the late 70s to early 90s, and the 'Public Choice'
> school of political analysis practised by right-wing think tanks.
> The market is viewed as correcting Government failures (rather
> than vice versa). No matter that, as in so many instances of
> privatisation (electricity, for example) the most intricate socio-
> economic engineering can only produce a market which is ar-
> tificial, rigged, imperfect and imperfectable. Nevertheless, the
> market is seen, uncritically, as a pseudo-natural phenomenon
> which substitutes for the exercise of collectively rational choice.
> The down-grading of rational choice based on analysis, then, is
> by no means an accidental, isolated phenomenon. It stems,
> rather, from the elevation of the market to almost divine, om-
> nipotent, omniscient status. (pp. 301–2)

Rosenhead was talking generally about the market, but all his criticisms
apply to education. In addition, education is even less a market than
Rosenhead's example of electricity — 'artificial, rigged', etc: schooling
is compulsory, 'perfect information' is completely lacking, and there is
not even a price mechanism available to regulate supply and demand.
It is a rigged non-market. We end up with the worst of both worlds —
a confused mixture of compulsion and competition, with more demand
for choice than can possibly be supplied. In education the idea of a
market is a non-starter; pretending that real choice exists for most parents
is dishonest.

The second view is a philosophical argument put convincingly by
Ruth Jonathan (1989). She begins by asking whether the benefit of
more choice for the consumer is sufficient to justify a policy change
which necessarily entails a retreat from a previous consensus commitment to social justice. She argues that the introduction of an internal
market into education, partly by encouraging parental choice, is likely

to produce greater diversity in the quality of schooling. She points out that there is a reluctance by policy-makers to evaluate the results of encouraging parental choice; instead, such policies have been introduced by appealing to individual parents' liberties, ignoring more general social consequences. Jonathan demonstrates that the status of parental rights is problematic and should not simply be taken for granted: she reiterates the classical distinction between moral and conventional (legal) rights, suggesting that the superficially strong case for moral rights is used to strengthen the conventional rights (by new legislation). Jonathan proceeds to differentiate between orders of rights — general, contractual and welfare — which have differing degrees of justificatory force, but in the current debate have not been differentiated. She shows that a right to education is neither a general nor a contractual right, and that as a welfare right it is claimed against the rights of other members of the community.

> A policy which gives individuals the opportunity for each to maximise her own holding in a competitive or market situation might indeed be expected to have harmful consequences for those individuals who, for whatever reason, are less effective in exploiting that opportunity. (p. 338)

To summarize this argument very crudely, I would suggest that what it amounts to in terms of the 1988 and 1993 Acts is that the Conservatives have argued the case for parental choice as though it were a straightforward absolute right, ignoring the complex case for balancing individual rights against other competing rights and the common good.

A third argument has been put forward by Stewart Ranson (1993a) who is less restrained in his critique of 'choice' and sees the issue as a clear-cut contrast — 'Markets or Democracy for Education'. Ranson sets out explicitly to oppose the Chubb and Moe arguments from the USA and those of Tooley (1992) in the UK. Ranson's position is that 'the mechanism of the market is intrinsically flawed as a vehicle for improving educational opportunities: it can only contract them' (p. 334). Basic to his argument is a rejection of the utilitarian assumption that individuals are entirely self-interested — a position which simply does not fit in with everyday experience; but the creation of some markets may make individuals more self-interested.

Ranson goes further and attacks the appropriateness of the market idea in education: the market usually assumes that a choice decision does not affect the commodity purchased; but this is manifestly not the case with schooling — the choice to send a child to a school (together with similar choices by many other parents) may change the character of the school. This in itself defeats the idea of the rationality of the market in education because a parent has to make a choice not knowing how many other parents will also choose the same.

> These seemingly unpredictable collective outcomes of private choice can create for any individual the disturbing effect of bringing into question the very rationality of action in the education market place. (p. 335)

Ranson also points out an intriguing paradox — that consumer choice empowers the producers: thus not only do schools begin to select parents, but having established a niche in the market, some schools specialize and important choices begin to disappear. 'The education market becomes the social manifestation of Darwinian natural selection' (p. 337). Furthermore, the fittest are curiously defined by the Right in terms of social hierarchy; politicians pretend to assume that all parents have equal access to the market but to lack these resources — cars, time or even the ability to move house — is to be 'disenfranchised from the polity of the market . . . the market is formally neutral but substantively interested . . . under the guise of neutrality, the institution of the market actively confirms and reinforces the pre-existing social class order of wealth and privilege' (p. 337).

This 'market' is not the natural, spontaneous phenomenon of right-wing tracts about the hidden hand, but a political creation designed to redistribute power (away from LEAs) and redirect society from social democracy towards a neo-liberal order. 'The market in education is not the classical market of perfect competition but an administered market carefully regulated with stringent controls' (p. 338). Democratic discussion within a community is replaced by this phoney market.

Ranson accuses the New Right of being either naive or dishonest — either not understanding the evidence or deliberately developing a rhetoric of choice to bamboozle the public. In this Paper he offers instead an attractive vision of a 'learning society' in which openness and active citizenship would be prized. It is an alternative that is unlikely to be adopted by Conservatives.

There is another paradox here: I have shown in earlier chapters that the Tories tend to be over concerned with tradition, yet they have, during the years 1979–94, continued to misread history so badly. They failed to perceive that Victorian values did not support minimal government and unbridled market licence, but were concerned to restrain the excesses of nineteenth-century *laissez-faire* economics. They seemed to ignore the major contribution of Disraeli to Conservative ideology — that is the moderating influence of paternalist, one-nation Toryism.

Marquand (1994) has pointed out another important contradiction:

> The capitalist free market is inherently, quintessentially subversive. It is the enemy of tradition, of stability, of establishments, of deference — of anything that restrains individual appetites. It says that Jack, provided Jack has money in his pocket, is as good as his master; that push-pin, to use Bentham's famous comparison, is as good as poetry. Because of this the gales of creative destruction which have punctuated its history, and which spur it on to ever more conquests, are far more disruptive than anything dreamed of by the socialist left. (*The Guardian*, 17 January 1994)

It is understandable that the populist Margaret Thatcher missed this point, but how could Quinton have ignored such a serious contradiction in the lecture discussed earlier in this chapter? Should he not have been just as critical of the neo-liberal position as he was of left-progressivism? Both Quinton and O'Hear seem to have chosen to turn a blind eye to the defective arguments of their allies within the Party.

Unfortunately that kind of lack of historical and cultural awareness is typical. And if some Conservatives are aware of the contradictions, most have remained silent. The few who have protested, for example, Ian Gilmour, have been ignored. An exception is the conservative philosopher, John Gray (1993) who makes the obvious but important point that imperfectability also applies to markets — markets are as fallible as any other human institution — and the market is only one dimension of a society in which individuals make choices and exercise responsibility.

Gray also accuses the New Right of three further crimes against Conservatism. First, the New Right has brought into Conservative discourse a sectarian spirit that belongs properly not with Conservatism but with rationalist doctrines of the Enlightenment, applying principles rather than seeking consensus. Second, the New Right has neglected the common culture, reducing everything to a 'calculus of exchange', forgetting that markets are legal artefacts; the New Right evades the issue of legitimacy that market institutions must possess. Finally, Gray criticizes the neglect of history by the New Right who instead repose trust in legalistic and constitutional devices.

Gray concludes that neo-liberal ideas were a useful antidote to statism, but have distracted attention from the central concerns of traditional Conservatism. A *laissez-faire* model is utopian; the real answer for Gray is a market controlled by government (which is limited but not minimal) and a modernized welfare state.

Meanwhile the market experiment is clearly damaging the education system: for example, classes are getting larger, schools are now appointing young inexperienced staff because they cannot afford those with experience, and the gap between good and bad schools is widening.

The Prospect of a Conservative Plan for Education

Sooner or later it will become obvious that the idea of a market in education is nonsense. Large industrial organizations plan their training programmes with care; any modern nation must plan both training and education. At some point the Conservatives will revert, more or less reluctantly, to educational planning. How successful are they likely to be? Given the characteristics of the Tory Mind in the post-Thatcher era, what are the problems likely to be in their attempting to plan for the second half of the 1990s and the twenty-first century?

The answer must be that the difficulties for Tory planners will be enormous. The crucial factor is that, as we have seen in earlier chapters, the UK is already lagging far behind other countries in many significant respects, and even much less-developed members of the European Community, such as Greece, Spain and Portugal, are overtaking us on some education criteria. Our competitors are not likely to call a halt to their programmes in education and training while we catch up. An effective plan for the UK would need to be bold and forward-looking, and it would be costly. A major obstacle for the Conservatives is, as we have seen, that the Tory Mind is essentially cautious, backward-looking and parsimonious towards education. They regret many developments of the modern world and prefer a more stable world picture some time in the past — myths are very powerful.

There are, of course, times when retrenchment and stability are advantageous. But there are other times when they may drag a society down, particularly in the sphere of education. For example, General Franco may have contributed a good deal to the stability of Spain after the destructive civil war 1936–39; his conservatism at that time may have given Spain a period of much needed stability. But the time came when what the country needed was a better quality education service and this Franco could not provide, because his brand of conservatism was firmly focused on the past rather than the future. Only when he died was it possible for priority to be given to planning a modern education service. Had Franco lived longer, the education reforms introduced under Juan Carlos would not have been possible: Franco would have considered them too costly, even undesirable — probably subversive. There are many other examples of reactionary regimes failing to reform education, although they wanted to modernize other aspects of their society — for example, Greece under the colonels or Brazil under the military junta.

Planning for the future by looking back nostalgically is a recipe for disaster in education. Moreover, the Tory mind is over-concerned with hierarchies and elites at a time when high priority should be given to education and training *for all*. This does not mean, of course, that we can afford to neglect the most able of our young people, but the evidence is that our existing system fails those lower down the scale socially and intellectually (see the NCE Report). The Tory obsession with class, differentiation and selection makes it difficult for them to plan for the majority. A classic example is their long-standing desire to hang on to the 'A' Level failure system when educationists and industrialists have for twenty years been pleading for a broader curriculum and a more integrated approach to education 16–19. There has never been a Conservative Party document which looks at this problem constructively in the way that the IPPR (Finegold, 1990) or the CBI (1989) have. The Tory Mind finds it difficult to escape from obsolete notions of knowledge, standards and achievement.

Further evidence of the difficulties faced by Conservative planners could be provided by a detailed account of the reform of the curriculum 5–16 since the 1988 Act. There is no space here for detail, but the following summary of mistakes may be sufficient.

1 The Baker National Curriculum was itself badly designed. Significantly the ten foundation subjects looked back to 1904 rather than forward to the 1990s.
2 The Conservative modernizers were also impeded by backward-looking privatizers and minimalists who were doubtful about even the most modest reform being suggested.
3 National Curriculum assessment procedures were bedeviled by the Tory desire for traditional tests when better assessment instruments were available, but they would have involved trusting teacher assessment, which was unacceptable.
4 The progressive 'entitlement' National Curriculum gradually gave

way to old-fashioned notions of 'core plus options' which had been shown by HMI to be unsatisfactory in the 1970s.

A potentially modernizing curriculum reform was predictably bungled by a mixture of incompetence, reactionary prejudice and suspicion. The cost in financial and human terms has been enormous.

Another example of difficulty for future Conservative education planners is the whole question of organizing the education service. I have mentioned above that the 1988 Act pursued a policy of devolving authority to the schools and at the same time moving towards much greater centralization. This contradiction has resulted in widespread confusion. One of the objectives was to remove educational power (and spending) from local authority control. A feature of education organization until 1988 was partnership; the whittling away of LEA responsibilities and the setting up of new quangos reporting to the Secretary of State alone has in effect given tremendous powers of control to the government of the day. A state of affairs which until recently was thought to be 'un-British and un-Tory'. There are two suggested explanations for this apparently confused policy: the first justifies more central power as a method of balancing the much greater local control in the hands of governors; the second is that the central power is intended to be temporary — once *all* schools are free from LEAs, then they will control themselves within a market and central power will become unnecessary. This sounds just about as unlikely as the withering away of the state in Marxist theory. It has been suggested that this kind of Conservative centralization is a reversion to nineteenth-century patronage which prevailed until the Northcote-Trevellyan reforms of 1853–54 — but now the patronage is on a much greater scale.

The NCE Report obviously spotted some of the dangers of this new centralization and proposed the creation of new local bodies — Education and Training Boards (ETBs). To parallel the innovation, they recommended a new central authority for education *and* training — the Department of Education and Training (DET). These proposals are unacceptable to the Tory Mind for several reasons. First, Conservatives prefer to keep education and training quite separate and distinct for ideological reasons; second, establishing ETBs with real powers and responsibilities would be seen as a U-turn after the deliberate campaign to emasculate LEAs; third, bringing education and training together, nationally and locally, would make the Tory stance on 'A' Levels, and the separation of academic and vocational much weaker. Tory thinking on general education, vocational education and training is particularly unsatisfactory (see Finegold *et al.*, 1992–93).

Stewart Ranson (1993b) has, in a separate document for NCE, commented on the completely unsatisfactory nature of the present arrangements and the difficulty of either operating it successfully or changing it in a rational way. This difficulty is related to the overall policy of leaving as much as possible to market forces. The result is that we have a compromise which is a muddle. Ranson argues for a 'learning society' in which local democratic planning would have a crucial part to play. It is quite different from anything being suggested by the Conservative Party:

> The current political system encourages passive rather than active participation in the public domain. A different order of values, giving all people a firm sense of purpose in their lives, can create the conditions for motivation in the classroom. It would encourage individuals to value their active role as citizens and thus their shared responsibility for the common-wealth. Active learning in the classroom needs, therefore, to be informed by and to lead towards citizenship within a participative democracy. (Ranson, 1993b, p. 4)

In the UK the only chance for a successful Conservative education plan would be for the moderate pluralists to vanquish the reactionary and nostalgic privatizers and minimalists in the Party, and to secure large additional funds for the education service. This is an unlikely prospect and even if it happened, the doubts would remain. The most successful Tory Ministers from the past would now fail: a Rab Butler could not produce the plan we now need, nor could Eccles — they were both much too dominated by tradition. Boyle might have succeeded, but even that is by no means certain. The safest assumption is that if the Conservatives win the next election, we should be ready to face a further period of educational confusion together with policies quite inappropriate for the twenty-first century.

Our real need is to develop a programme of modernization which is not only economic but concerned with more general cultural modernization, including education. Educational change will be part of modernization but will also be a prerequisite for other desirable changes. The Tory Mind will keep us in the past when we need both respect for tradition *and* the ability to innovate away from tradition when necessary. We cannot predict what changes will take place, or when they will take place, but we can have some ideas about the kind of changes that will be necessary, and we can make sure that the education service will make it possible for them to happen.

Part IV

Conclusion

Part IV consists of one final chapter. Chapter 9 returns to the central question introduced in the first chapter: the nature of the Tory Mind. Five traditional Conservative beliefs and attitudes are examined, and related to education.

The dominant attitude is found to be an exaggerated concern for traditions; but they tend to be dead traditions. Other related key concepts are a desire for more selection; a dislike of experts and theory; a concern about spending too much on education; a bias in favour of appealing to parental choice and market forces; and a constant pressure to reduce LEA powers by increasing central control.

The other major finding of the study is the curious Tory belief in a left-wing, educational establishment plot to subvert education.

Finally, it is found that traditional Tory values have been distorted by Hayekian neo-liberal beliefs in a free market to such an extent that it will be difficult for the Conservative Party to develop any coherent plan for the education service in the twenty-first century.

Chapter 9

Summary and Conclusion

Hayek's famous book *The Road to Serfdom.* . . . is instructive here. . . . As Herman Finer pointed out in his *Road to Reaction*, Hayek allows no compromise or moderation; his book is an anti-democratic, quasi-dictatorial tract, intolerant of countervailing institutions. Nothing is to stand in the way of the free market, and no such fripperies as democratic votes are to be allowed to upset it. The unadulterated free market is unalterable, and those who dislike it or suffer from it must learn to put up with it. In Rousseau's language, they must be forced to be free. (Ian Gilmour, p. 223)

There was the need to go much further with 'opting out' of LEA control. I authorised John MacGregor to announce to the October 1990 Party Conference the extension of the GM schools scheme to cover smaller primary schools as well. But I had much more radical options in mind. Brian Griffiths had written me a Paper which envisaged the transfer of many more schools to GM status and the transfer of other schools — which were not yet ready to assume the full responsibility — to the management of special trusts, set up for the propose. Essentially, this would have meant the unbundling of many of the LEA's powers, leaving them with a monitoring and advisory role — perhaps in the long term not even that. (Thatcher, p. 597)

This book has attempted to deal with three questions:

* What is the nature of the Tory Mind, and, in particular, Tory attitudes to education?
* Did both kinds of attitude change between 1979 and 1994?
* If so, were they connected with Tory education policies during that period?

In other words, I have attempted to relate policies to belief systems and ideologies.

In chapter 1, I reviewed the ideas of some Conservative thinkers and politicians, and from it derived a more or less coherent picture which I will now summarize, under five headings, as 'traditional Conservative attitudes and beliefs', all of which influence attitudes to education:

human nature;
society;
moral values and behaviour;
knowledge;
technology.

I will say a little about each of them.

The traditional Conservative view of *human nature* has tended towards the Hobbesian view that human beings have strong instincts which need to be kept under control by the collective action of others. Without the order imposed by society, life would be nasty, brutish and short. Human beings are prone to crime and must be restrained by discipline and punishment. The socialization process may transform them from being lazy and selfish to becoming industrious and cooperative. The socialization process operates at various levels: the family, community and country (patriotism needs to be taught). Rousseau's view of the innocent child corrupted by an imperfect society is rejected in favour of the notion of sinful creatures transformed into useful citizens by correct upbringing, discipline and education (broadly defined).

The Conservative view of *society* follows from the view of human nature. Society is not an utopia where everyone can do whatever they wish; it is an orderly, hierarchical structure in which individuals learn their place and practise their duties, and obligations within various groups in society. Strong forces of law and order are essential in order to preserve the stability of that hierarchical structure which includes a reasonably flexible class system. Part of that stable social structure is the economic system. Conservative thought has moved, over the centuries, further away from semi-feudal attitudes to land as the major factor in the hierarchy to a more pure class system based on wealth and income. But, as we have seen, feudal vestiges remain important in society and in the Tory Mind. Politically, democracy is regarded as a necessary outcome of nineteenth-century social and economic change. The Conservative genius has enabled them to retain power and as much of the status quo as possible, by manipulating the democratic machinery with maximum subtlety.

At the time of Disraeli the traditional Conservative view of *moral values and behaviour* was orthodox Christianity as exemplified by the

Church of England, combined with a pragmatic rationality based to some extent on science and also the examples of great lives derived mainly from Latin and Greek authors. As the nineteenth century gave way to the twentieth, scientific thinking loomed larger. Personal morality was based on the family and loyalty to other groups such as school, regiment, club and class.

The Conservative view of *knowledge* is based on 'common sense' pragmatism — what works. But there is a paradox: knowledge is seen as sharply divided into specialist areas of expertise — the law, medicine and, at a lower level, school subjects such as history, mathematics and science. Yet the gentleman amateur ideal demands general knowledge rather than too much expertise in one area. Experts with theories should be treated with suspicion — even hostility.

Technology is to be differentiated from knowledge. Technology is seen as the practical application of certain kinds of knowledge such as science. It is good because it is useful; but it is to be treated with suspicion because it is often unfamiliar, innovative and potentially disruptive of the social order. Several writers such as Barnett and Wiener have commented that upper-class thinking, conservative thinking, has given technology and related occupations such as engineering low status.

This traditional conservative view was, I suggest, a coherent ideology. But it was under threat in the 1960s and 1970s. By 1979 it was being contaminated by neo-liberal ideas which made conservatism less coherent and more open to charges of contradiction. It would be unwise to exaggerate changes that have taken place among only some Conservatives or to overemphasize the importance for the Party as a whole. Nevertheless, it is clear that changes have taken place and that what were minority views among Tory MPs have become very influential, perhaps dominant. I will briefly describe these neo-liberal influences, using the same five headings as before.

On *human nature* the Hobbesian view is still important but has been replaced to some extent by ideas of Adam Smith and Hayek. There is still an emphasis on the strong, but limited, state, law and order, and the class structure, but — significantly — individualism has tended to replace community values.

On *society*, the market as a 'hidden hand' has become much more important and is not confined to narrowly economic matters; it has spread to any sphere where individual choice within a market appears to solve problems of distribution. The market has tended to replace notions of 'fairness' which is a traditional community value rather than a feature of individualism. The class system remains important but has tended to become more meritocratic at the expense of social stability.

Moral values and behaviour The balance between Christianity and science has moved, so that modern neo-liberal Conservatives are sometimes guilty of scientism. For some the gospel according to Friedman and Hayek is more important than traditional Christian values such as compassion, charity or 'love thy neighbour'. The market looms large as a god-like dominating force. Morality has become more a question of individual beliefs (even taste) than consensus or community norms.

The traditional view of *knowledge* has proved very resilient, except that utility or 'usefulness' as a criterion of importance has gained at the expense of cultural heritage.

Technology Conservative modernizers are sometimes fascinated by technology and information technology, to such an extent that they become more important than people.

The Tory Mind is a reflection of *Zeitgeist* — the spirit of the age — as well as shaping it, to some extent. But the Tory Mind is also a product of history: of the democratization of England since Disraeli; of the loss of Empire since 1945. Their preferred solution is to look back and seek inspiration from traditional culture, but since 1979 the culture of Conservatism has itself changed.

*   *   *

The dominant feature of the Tory Mind that has emerged from this study is, unsurprisingly, an exaggerated concern for tradition and past models of education and society. But what did surprise me when reading so many speeches and autobiographies was the Tory *fear* of the future and of the non-traditional. I was even more surprised by the kind of fear which took the form of an almost paranoid belief in conspiracies among the 'educational establishment'. It becomes clear that this has distorted the Tory perception of education in ways which would be amusing if they did not have such serious consequences for the education system — for example, teachers could not be trusted to assess their own pupils for National Curriculum Key Stages 1 to 3 and this wasted about £500 million!

I have, in chapter 3, commented on Margaret Thatcher's (1993) reference to the anti-enterprise culture that had taken root in the DES (p. 151) and Keith Joseph's view of an 'unholy alliance' of socialists, bureaucrats, planners and Directors of Education which Knight (1990), a Tory supporter himself, claims was shared by 'all Conservative educationists' (p. 155). According to Knight, Joseph's view was that the 'unholy alliance' was acting against the true interests of the nation's children. (See discussion in chapter 3 above.) Even the more moderate Kenneth Baker (1993) complained about the views of his senior civil servants in a similar way, accusing them of being in league with the teacher unions, University Departments of Education, LEAs and HMI. (p. 168). Kenneth Clarke dismissed the views of teachers and education theorists as left wing (see the criticism by Black, 1992, discussed in chapter 6); and after John Patten became Secretary of State, the government was criticized by the recently retired Senior Chief Inspector for ignoring the views of all except those on the extreme Right. And it was wild accusations by John Major, for which he was unable to provide any evidence, which generated the lengthy Jarvis–Major correspondence that I summarized in chapter 5.

Had all of these remarks been made in such contexts as the Conservative Party Conference, then one might be tempted to put them aside as mere political rhetoric designed to rekindle fires in the bellies of the faithful and not meant to be taken seriously outside those emotional gatherings. But this was not the case, and unbiased observers would, I am sure, come to the conclusion — having examined all the evidence — that Tories really do seem to believe in the existence of left-wing, 'education establishment' conspiracies which have as their purpose deliberately distorting the education of children who go through the state education system.

To anyone who knows the system this belief is clearly absurd; and if there were any truth in the allegations, there would surely be some evidence available rather than just the suspicions which have been given prominence by much of the Tory press. In some respects this kind of paranoia has features in common with the series of rumours which circulated about Harold Wilson when he was Prime Minister. It was suggested, on the flimsiest of 'evidence' that Wilson was a Russian spy and that Gaitskell had been murdered in order to make way for Wilson as leader of the Labour Party (Pimlott, 1992). An independent inquiry into that whole story by David Leigh (1988) clearly demolished the allegation, but Leigh also showed that sections of the Right (including Peter Wright of *Spycatcher* fame) believed the story and some even linked it to other right-wing myths such as the supposed Jewish/Zionist plot to destroy Western civilization!

In retrospect, the Wilson-as-Russian-spy story seems incredible, but the allegations about 'producer domination' by a political consortium of teachers, university departments of education, Chief Education Officers and Her Majesty's Inspectors are equally absurd. This book has not attempted to provide any kind of psychological explanation for the 'unconscious' Tory Mind but has concentrated on the investigation of evidence on the surface. At this level — that is, what Tories actually say and write — there are links between unbalanced regard for tradition, fear of the future, unwillingness to upset existing class structures, dislike of a changing educational system and irrational fears of 'producer-capture'. In chapter 6 I summarized the evidence on the Tory Mind on education under six value positions:

* a desire for more selection;
* a wish to return to traditional curricula and teaching methods;
* a desire to reduce the influence of experts and educational theory;'
* an appeal to parental choice to encourage market forces;
* a wish to reduce educational expenditure;
* a process of increased centralization (and reducing LEA power/ influence).

In 1994 we are now a long way away from the educational consensus of the 1940s and 1950s where pluralist policies appeared to have won the day. The Tory Mind of the 1980s and 1990s has, instead, revived minimalist and privatizer attitudes and beliefs which, combined with weird conspiracy theories, become dangerously reactionary. I am not, of course, suggesting that all Conservatives hold these views — Heath, Gilmour and Thornton are by no means alone in regretting Thatcherite developments — only that they have become dominant in the rhetoric of Rightish educational discourse and have had an important influence on Tory policies.

This may also help to explain why the hitherto non-Tory idea of the free market has become so central to Conservative social thinking in general and to education policies in particular. The market may have appeared to the Right to be the only alternative to educational planning which would, by definition, be in the hands of the 'enemy'. In the nineteenth century *laissez-faire* was a Whig–Liberal belief which was rejected by Conservative leaders from Disraeli onwards. They saw that the unfettered market ran counter to traditional, paternalistic, one-nation Toryism. The Thatcherite 'market solution' is a dramatic change in direction for Toryism. Almost as surprising as the Tory conspiracy theory is conversion to the belief that market forces can be relied upon to produce the kind of social system needed for the twenty-first century, including education. Not only is this contrary to all the evidence, it is unsupported by even one example of a society where such an education policy has been successfully employed. And, as Rosenhead (1992) has pointed out, the market is potentially a destructive force within traditional society. The present is characterized by many contradictions.

The Future

If the Tory Mind in its present form is given control of education for the twenty-first century, we will have a combination of backward-looking attitudes, exaggerated beliefs in traditions, bolstering up a class system by various selective devices, spending too little money on education and rejecting modern methods and technological improvements; the education service will remain in the grip of an over-centralized, bureaucratic machine.

Some hoped that when John Major replaced Margaret Thatcher there would be a move away from this mixture of exaggerated traditionalism, market forces and over-centralization in education. This has proved not to be the case and arguments in support of Tory education policies have in some ways declined in quality. Unless another Disraeli appears to play the role of wizard, saving his country as well as his Party, the attack on the education service is likely to continue. The prospect for education is bleak, unless. . . .

Bibliography

ADDISON, P. (1993) 'Destiny, history and providence: The religion of Winston Churchill', in Bentley, M. (Ed) *Public and Private Doctrine*, Cambridge, Cambridge University Press.

ADLER, M. (1993) *An Alternative Approach to Parental Choice*, NCE Briefing 13.

ADLER, M. *et al.* (1989) *Parental Choice and Educational Policy*, Edinburgh, Edinburgh University Press.

ALPORT, C. *et al.* (1950) *One Nation: A Tory Approach to Social Problems*, London, Conservative Political Centre.

BAKER, K. (1993) *The Turbulent Years: My Life in Politics*, London, Faber.

BALDWIN, S. (1938) *On England*, London, Hodder and Stoughton.

BALL, C. (1990) *More Means Different*, London, Royal Society of Arts.

BALL, C. (1991) *Learning Pays*, London, Royal Society of Arts.

BALL, S. (1990) *Politics and Policy Making in Education*, London, Routledge.

BARNETT, C. (1996) *The Audit of War*, London, Macmillan.

BENN, A. (1989) *Diaries*, Hutchinson.

BENNETT, N. (1976) *Teaching Styles and Pupil Progress*, Open Books.

BENTLEY, M. (Ed) (1993) *Public and Private Doctrine*, Cambridge, Cambridge University Press.

BLACK, P. (1992) *Education: Putting the Record Straight*, Network.

BLACK, P. (1993) 'The shifting scenery of the National Curriculum', in CHITTY, C. and SIMON, B. (Eds) *Education Answers Back*, Lawrence and Wishart, pp. 45–60.

BLAKE, R. (1985) *The Conservative Party From Peel to Thatcher*, London, Fontana.

BOLTON, E. (1992) 'Imaginary gardens with real toads', reprinted in CHITTY, C. and SIMON, B. (Eds) *Education Answers Back*, Lawrence and Wishart, pp. 3–16.

BOSANQUET, N. (1983) *After the New Right*, Heinemann.

BOYLE, E. (1970) 'The politics of secondary school reorganisation: Some reflections', *Journal of Educational Administration and History*, 4, 2, pp. 28–38.

BOYLE, E. (1976) *Parliament's Views on Responsibility for Education Policy Since 1944*, Alfred G. Mays Memorial Lecture, Institute of Local Government Studies, University of Birmingham.

BOYLE, E. and CROSLAND, A. (1971) (in conversation with M. Kogan) *The Politics of Education*, Penguin.

BOYSON, R. (Ed) (1970) *Right Turn*, London, Churchill Press.

BOYSON, R. (Ed) (1972) *Education: Threatened Standards*, London, Churchill Press.

BROWN, M. (1993) *Clashing Epistemologies: The Battle for Control of the National Curriculum and its Assessment*, Inaugural Lecture, London, Kings College.

BUTLER, R. A. (1971) *The Art of the Possible*, Harmondsworth, Penguin.

BUTLER, R. A. (1982) *The Art of Memory*, Hodder and Stoughton.

CBI (1989) *Towards a Skills Revolution*, London, Confederation of British Industry.

CHITTY, C. (1989) *Towards a New Education System: The Victory of the New Right?*, Lewes, Falmer Press.

CHITTY, C. (Ed) (1993) *The National Curriculum: Is It Working?*, Longman.

CHITTY, C. and SIMON, B. (Eds) (1993) *Education Answers Back*, Lawrence and Wishart.

CHUBB, J. E. and MOE, T. M. (1990) *Politics, Markets, and American Schools* Washington D.C., Brookings Institute.

CHUBB, J. E. and MOE, T. M. (1992) *A Lesson in School Reform from Great Britain*, Washington D.C., Brookings Institute.

CHURCHILL, P. and MITCHELL, J. (1974) *Jennie: Lady Randolph Churchill — A Portrait with Letters*, Fontana.

CLARK, A. (1993) *Diaries*, Weidenfeld and Nicolson.

CLARKE, K. (1991a) speech to North of England Conference (Leeds), DFE.

CLARKE, K. (1991b) Westminster Lecture, Conservative Central Office.

CLARKE, K. (1992) speech to North of England Conference (Southport), DFE.

CODD, J. A. (1988) 'The construction and deconstruction of educational policy documents', *Journal of Educational Policy*, 3, 3, pp. 235–47.

CONSERVATIVE PARTY (1974) *Manifesto*, London.

CONSERVATIVE PARTY (1976) *The Right Approach*, London.

CONSERVATIVE PARTY (1979) *Manifesto*, London.

CONSERVATIVE PARTY (1983) *Manifesto*, London.

COX, C. B. (1992) *The Great Betrayal*, Chapmans.

COX, C. and MARKS, J. (1988) *The Insolence of Office*, Claridge Press.

COX, C. B. and BOYSON, R. (Eds) (1975) *Black Paper 1975: The Fight for Education*, Dent.

Cox, C. B. and Boyson, R. (Eds) (1977) *Black Paper 1977*, London, Maurice Temple Smith.

Cox, C. B. and Dyson, A. E. (Eds) (1969a) *Fight for Education: A Black Paper*, London, Critical Quarterly Society.

Cox, C. B. and Dyson, A. E. (Eds) (1969b) *Black Paper Two: The Crisis in Education*, Critical Quarterly Society.

Cox, C. B. and Dyson, A. E. (Eds) (1970) *Black Paper Three: Goodbye Mr Short*, Critical Quarterly Society.

Cox, C. B. and Dyson, A. E. (Eds) (1971) *The Black Papers on Education*, Davis-Poynter.

Darling-Hammond, L. *et al.* (1983) 'Teacher evaluation in the organisational context', *Review of Educational Research*, 53, 3, pp. 285–328.

Dean, D. (1992) 'Preservation or renovation? The dilemmas of Conservative Educational Policy 1955–1960', *20th Century British History*, 3, 1, pp. 3–31.

Dearing, R. (1993) *Final Report: The National Curriculum and its Assessment*, SCAA.

Department of Education and Science (1980a) *A Framework for the School Curriculum*, London, HMSO.

Department of Education and Science (1980b) *A View of the Curriculum*, London, HMSO.

Department of Education and Science (1981) *The School Curriculum*, London, HMSO.

Department of Education and Science (1983) *Teaching Quality*, London, HMSO.

Department of Education and Science (1985) *Better Schools*, London, HMSO.

Department of Education and Science (1988) *National Curriculum: The TGAT Report*, London, HMSO.

Department For Education (1992) *White Paper: Choice and Diversity*, London, HMSO.

Eccles, D. (1967) *Life and Politics: A Moral Diagnosis*, Longmans.

Eliot, T. S. (1955) *The Literature of Politics*, Conservative Political Centre.

Finegold, D. *et al.* (1990) *A British Baccalaureat*, London, IPPR.

Finegold, D. *et al.* (Eds) (1992–93) 'Something borrowed, something blue?', *Oxford Studies in Comparative Education* vol. 2 1992, vol. 3 1993, Wallingford, Oxford, Triangle Books, pp. 1–128.

Friedman, M. (1962) *Capitalism and Freedom*, Chicago, University of Chicago Press.

Galbraith, J. K. (1992) *The Culture of Contentment*, London, Sinclair-

Stevenson.

GARDNER, H. (1983) *Frames of Mind*, London, Fontana.

GELLNER, E. (1992) *Postmodernism, Reason and Religion*, Routledge.

GILMOUR, I. (1992) *Dancing With Dogma: Britain Under Thatcherism*, Simon and Schuster.

GOSDEN, P. (1976) *Education in the Second World War*, Methuen.

GOSDEN, P. (1983) *The Education System Since 1944*, Martin Robertson.

GOSDEN, P. (1985) 'Educational policy', in BELL, D. (Ed) *The Conservative Government 1979–84*, Croom Helm.

GRAHAM, D. (1992) PLATFORM Opinion article entitled 'Beware Hasty Changes'-Duncan Graham weighs up the achievements of the National Curriculum and argues for a Quality Assurance partnership *The Times Education Supplement*, 3, January 1992.

GRAHAM, D. (1993) 'The National Curriculum and the 14–19 Curriculum' in TOMLINSON, H. (Ed) *Education and Training 14–19*, Harlow, Longmans.

GRAHAM, D. and TYTLER, D. (1993) *A Lesson for us All: The Making of the National Curriculum*, Routledge.

GRAY, J. (1993) *Beyond the New Right*, Routledge.

GREEN, D. G. (1993) *Reinventing Civil Society*, IEA.

HAILSHAM, LORD (1990) *A Sparrow's Flight*, Fontana.

HALDANE, J. (Ed) (1992) *Education, Values and Culture: the Victor Cook Memorial Lectures*, St Andrews, University of St Andrews.

HALSEY, A. H. (1988) 'A sociologist's view of Thatcherism', in SKIDELSKY, R. (Ed) *Thatcherism*, London, Chatto and Windus, pp. 173–90.

HALSEY, A. H. (1992) *Opening Wide the Doors of Higher Education*, NCE Briefing 6.

HAVILAND, J. (1988) *Take Care Mr Baker! A Selection from the Advice on Education which the Government Collected, but Decided not to Publish*, London, Fourth Estate.

HAYEK, F. (1943) *The Road to Serfdom*, London, Routledge.

HEALEY, D. (1989) *The Time of My Life*, London, Michael Joseph.

HEATON, R. N. and GOODFELLOW, S. M. E. (1987) 'Preliminaries to the Act', *The Times Education Supplement*, 24 July 1987.

HIGGINSON, G. (1988) *Advancing 'A' Levels*, London, HMSO.

HILLGATE GROUP (1986) *Whose Schools?*, London, Hillgate Group.

HILLGATE GROUP (1987) *The Reform of British Education*, Claridge Press.

HILLGATE GROUP (1989) *Learning to Teach*, Claridge Press.

HORNE, A. (1988) *Macmillan* Vol. I 1894–1956, London, Macmillan.

HORNE, A. (1989) *Macmillan* Vol. II 1957–1986, London, Macmillan.

HOWARD, A. (1987) *Rab: the Life of R. A. Butler*, Cape.

JARVIS, F. (1993) *Education and Mr Major*, Tufnell Press.

JEFFEREYS, K. (1984) 'R. A. Butler, The Board of Education and the 1944 Education Act', *History*, 69, 227, pp. 415–31.

JONATHAN, R. (1989) 'Choice and control in education: Parental rights, individual liberties and social justice', *British Journal of Educational Studies*, 37, 4, pp. 321–38.

JONATHAN, R. (1990) 'State education service or prisoner's dilemma: The hidden hand as source of education policy', *British Journal of Educational Studies*, 38, 2, pp. 116–32.

JOSEPH, K. (1976) *Stranded on the Middle Ground*, London, Centre for Policy Studies.

JOSEPH, K. (1981) *'Good Schools for All'*, speech to Conservative Party Conference, Conservative Party Press Release.

JOSEPH, K. (1982) speech at North of England Conference, DES Press Release.

JOSEPH, K. (1984) speech at North of England Conference, DES Press Release.

JUDGE, H. (1984) *A Generation of Schooling*, Oxford, Oxford University Press.

KAVANAGH, D. (1987) *Thatcherism and British Politics: The End of Consensus?*, Oxford, Oxford University Press.

KINGDON, J. (1984) *Agendas, Alternatives and Public Policies*, Boston, Little and Brown.

KNIGHT, C. (1990) *The Making of Tory Education Policy in Post-War Britain 1950–1986*, Lewes, Falmer Press.

KOGAN, M. (1971) 'Introduction' to BOYLE, E. and CROSLAND, A. *The Politics of Education*, Harmondsworth, Penguin.

KOGAN, M. (1978) *The Politics of Educational Change*, Fontana.

KOGAN, M. (1989) 'Managerialism in higher education', in LAWTON, D. (Ed) *The ERA: Choice and Control*, London, Hodder and Stoughton.

LAWLOR, S. (1988) *Away with LEAs: ILEA Abolition as a Pilot*, London, Centre for Policy Studies.

LAWRENCE, I. (1992) *Power and Politics at the DES*, Cassell.

LAWSON, D., PLUMMERIDGE, C. and SWANWICK, K. (1993) *The National Curriculum: Music at Key Stages 1 and 2*. A Research Report. Institute of Education, University of London.

LAWSON, N. (1992) *The View From No. 11: Memoirs of a Tory Radical*, Corgi.

LAWTON, D. (1988) (Ed) *Choice and Control*, Hodder and Stoughton.

LAWTON, D. (1989) *Education, Culture and the National Curriculum*, Hodder and Stoughton.

LAWTON, D. (1992) *Education and Politics in the 1990s: Conflict or Consensus?*, London, Falmer Press.

LEIGH, D. (1988) *The Wilson Plot*, Heinemann.

LETWIN, O. (1988) *Privatising the World*, London, Cassell.

MACGREGOR, J. (1990) speech to Society of Education Officers' Conference.

MACGREGOR, J. (1991) 'The education debate' (The Swansea Speech) in WILLIAMS, M. *et al.* (Eds) *Continuing the Education Debate*, Cassell.

MACGREGOR, J. (1992) 'The education debate' in *ibid*.

MACLURE, S. (1989) *Education Re-Formed*, London, Hodder and Stoughton.

MCKENZIE, R. T. (1964) *British Political Parties*, Heinemann.

MCKIBBIN, R. (1990) 'The ideologies of class' in BENTLEY, M. (Ed) (1993) *Public and Private Doctrine: Essays to Maurice Cowling*, Cambridge, Cambridge University Press.

MAJOR, J. (1991) speech to Centre for Policy Studies, London, 10 Downing Street Press Release 3 July.

MAJOR, J. (1992a) Prime Minister's speech to Conservative Party Conference.

MAJOR, J. (1992b) speech to the Adam Smith Institute.

MAJOR, J. (1993) speech to Conservative Europe Group.

MARENBON, J. (1987) *English Our English: The New Orthodoxy Examined*, CPS.

MARQUAND, D. (1988a) 'The paradoxes of Thatcherism', in SKIDELSKY, R. (Ed) *Thatcherism*, London, Chatto and Windus, pp. 159–72.

MARQUAND, D. (1988b) *The Unprincipled Society*, Fontana.

MARQUAND, D. (1994) 'New Fashioned Humbug', in *The Guardian*, 17 January 1994.

MAUDE, A. (1968) *Education: Quality and Equality*, London, Conservative Political Centre.

MORGAN, K. O. (1990) *The Peoples' Peace*, Oxford.

MORTIMORE, P. and BLATCHFORD, P. (1993) *The Issue of Class Size*, NCE Briefing 12.

NATIONAL COMMISSION ON EDUCATION (1993) *Learning to Succeed*, Heinemann.

NISBET, R. (1986) *Conservatism*, Open University Press.

OAKESHOTT, M. (1989) 'Education: The Engagement and its Frustration', in *The Voice of Liberal Learning*, Yale University Press.

O'HEAR, A. (1988) *Who Teaches the Teachers?*, London, The Social Affairs Unit.

O'HEAR, A. (1992) 'The Victor Cook memorial lectures', in HALDANE, J. (Ed) *Education, Values and Culture*, St Andrews, University of St Andrews.

O'HEAR, P. and WHITE, J. (Eds) (1993) *Assessing the National Curriculum*, Paul Chapman.

O'KEEFFE, D. (1990) *The Wayward Elite*, London, ASI.

PATTEN, J. (1992) speech to Conservative Party Conference. (Reprinted in CHITY, C. and SIMON, B. (Eds) *Education Answers Back*, London, Lawrence and Wishart, pp. 145–52.

PATTEN, J. (1994) speech to Oxford Conference 5 January DFE Press Release.

PETERS, R. S. (Ed) (1968) *Perspectives on Plowden*, Routledge.

PILE, W. (1979) *The Department of Education and Science*, Allen and Unwin.

PIMLOTT, B. (1992) *Harold Wilson*, Harper Collins.

PRAIS, S. J. and WAGNER, K. (1983) *Schooling Standards in Britain and Germany*, NIESR.

PRIOR, J. (1986) *A Balance of Power*, Hamish Hamilton.

PYM, F. (1984) *The Politics of Consent*, Hamish Hamilton.

QUINTON, A. (1978) *The Politics of Imperfection: The Religious and Secular Traditions of Conservative Thought in England from Hooker to Oakeshott*, Faber and Faber.

RANSON, S. (1993a) 'Markets or democracy for education', *British Journal of Educational Studies*, xxxxi, 4, pp. 333–52.

RANSON, S. (1993b) *Local Democracy for the Learning Society*, NCE Briefing 18.

ROSENHEAD, J. (1992) 'Into the swamp: The analysis of social issues', *Journal of Operational Research Society*, 43, 4, pp. 293–305.

ROSS, J. (1983) *Thatcher and Friends: The Anatomy of the Tory Party*, Pluto Press.

RUMBOLD, A. (1989) speech to 'A' Level Conference, London, DES, November, Press Release.

SCHWEINHART, L. J. and WEIKART, D. P. (1993) 'A Summary of "Significant Benefits: the High/Scope Perry Pre-School Study"', High/Scope UK.

SCRUTON, R. (1980) *The Meaning of Conservatism*, London, Macmillan.

SCRUTON, R. (1982) *A Dictionary of Political Thought*, London, Macmillan.

SCRUTON, R. *et al.* (1985) *Education and Indoctrination*, London, Education Research Centre.

SEXTON, S. (1987) *Our Schools: A Radical Policy*, London, IEA.

SEXTON, S. (Ed) (1988) *GCSE*, London, IEA.

SEXTON, S. (Ed) (1990) *General Certificate of Secondary Education*, London, IEA.

SIMON, B. (1991) *Education and the Social Order 1940–1990*, London, Lawrence and Wishart.

SKIDELSKY, R. (Ed) (1988) *Thatcherism*, London, Chatto and Windus.

ST JOHN-STEVAS, N. (1977) *Better Schools for All: A Conservative Approach to the Problems of the Comprehensive School*, CPC.

THATCHER, M. (1993) *The Downing Street Years*, Harper Collins.

THORNTON, M. (1992) 'The role of the government in education', in CHITTY, C. and SIMON, B. (Eds) *Education Answers Back*, London, Lawrence and Wishart.

TOMLINSON, H. (Ed) (1993) *Education and Training 14–19*, Longmans.

TOOLEY, J. (1992) 'The prisoner's dilemma and educational provision: A reply to Ruth Jonathan', *British Journal of Educational Studies*, 40, 2, pp. 118–33.

VERNON, P. E. (1969) *Intelligence and Cultural Environment*, Methuen.

WALFORD, G. (1992) *Selection for Secondary Schooling*, NCE Briefing 7.

WALLACE, A. (1990) *Schools Out*, The Adam Smith Institute.

WALLACE, R. G. (1981) 'The origins and authorship of the 1944 education act', *History of Education*, 10, 4, pp. 238–90.

WAPSHOTT, N. and BROCK, G. (1983) *Thatcher*, Macdonald/Futura.

WELLS, H. G. (1934) *Experiment in Autobiography*, London, Gollancz.

WHITELAW, W. (1989) *The Whitelaw Memoirs*, Headline.

WIENER, M. (1985) *English Culture and the Decline of the Industrial Spirit 1850–1980*, Harmondsworth, Penguin.

WILLIAMS, M. *et al.* (Eds) (1992) *Continuing the Education Debate*, Cassell.

WILLIAMS, R. (1961) *The Long Revolution*, Harmondsworth, Penguin.

WILLMS, J. and ECHOLS, F. (1992) 'Alert and Inert Clients', *Economics of Education Review*, 11, 4, pp. 339–50.

WOOD, D. (1993) *The Classroom of 2015*, NCE Briefing 20.

WRIGHT, P. (1987) *Spycatcher*, Heinemann.

YOUNG, H. (1989) *One of Us*, London, Macmillan.

Index